EXCEL FOR WINDOWS FOR DUMMIES™

Quick Reference

2nd Edition

by John Walkenbach

IDG BOOKS

IDG Books Worldwide, Inc.
An International Data Group Company

San Mateo, California ♦ Indianapolis, Indiana ♦ Boston, Massachusetts

Excel For Dummies Quick Reference, Second Edition

Published by
IDG Books Worldwide, Inc.
An International Data Group Company
155 Bovet Road, Suite 310
San Mateo, CA 94402

Library of Congress Catalog Card No.: 94-75048

ISBN: 1-56884-096-9

Printed in the United States of America

10 9 8 7 6 5 4 3 2 1

Distributed in the United States by IDG Books Worldwide, Inc.

Distributed in Canada by Macmillan of Canada, a Division of Canada Publishing Corporation; by Computer and Technical Books in Miami, Florida, for South America and the Caribbean; by Longman Singapore in Singapore, Malaysia, Thailand, and Korea; by Toppan Co. Ltd. in Japan; by Asia Computerworld in Hong Kong; by Woodslane Pty. Ltd. in Australia and New Zealand; and by Transword Publishers Ltd. in the U.K. and Europe.

For information on where to purchase IDG Books outside the U.S., contact Christina Turner at 415-312-0633.

For information on translations, contact Marc Jeffrey Mikulich, Foreign Rights Manager, at IDG Books Worldwide; FAX NUMBER 415-358-1260.

For sales inquiries and special prices for bulk quantities, write to the address above or call IDG Books Worldwide at 415-312-0650.

is a trademark of IDG Books Worldwide, Inc.

COMPUTER
BOOK SERIES
FROM IDG

Acknowledgments

Thanks to everyone at IDG Books who helped transform hundreds of thousands of bytes on my hard disk into a real book: Janna Custer for choosing me to write it, Diane Steele and Sara Black for editing it, and all the others behind the scenes who pulled it all together. Thanks also to John Kaufeld for a superb technical review and to the production staff for making it look good. I would also like to acknowledge my friend Marisa, who is well on her way to becoming a computer nerd — and plays a mean game of Tetris. I appreciate the help from Sandra Pace at Waggener Edstrom for supplying me with a seemingly endless stream of Excel 5 betas. Finally, I would like to acknowledge Microsoft's Excel 5 development team for creating the world's best spreadsheet. You folks done good!

John Walkenbach
La Jolla, California

(The publisher would like to give special thanks to Patrick J. McGovern, without whom this book would not have been possible.)

Credits

Publisher
David Solomon

Managing Editor
Mary Bednarek

Acquisitions Editor
Janna Custer

Production Director
Beth Jenkins

Senior Editors
Tracy L. Barr
Sandra Blackthorn
Diane Graves Steele

Production Coordinator
Cindy L. Phipps

Acquisitions Assistant
Megg Bonar

Editorial Assistant
Darlene Cunningham

Editor
Sara Black

Technical Reviewer
John Kaufeld

Production Staff
Tony Augsburger
Valery Bourke
Mary Breidenbach
Chris Collins
Sherry Gomoll
Drew Moore
Kathie Schnorr
Gina Scott

Proofreader
Sandy Grieshop

Indexer
Sherry Massey

Cover Illustration
Kavish + Kavish

Say What You Think!

Listen up, all you readers of IDG's international bestsellers: the one — the only — absolutely world famous ...*For Dummies* books! It's time for you to take advantage of a new, direct pipeline to the authors and editors of IDG Books Worldwide. In between putting the finishing touches on the next round of ...*For Dummies* books, the authors and editors of IDG Books Worldwide like to sit around and mull over what their readers have to say. And we know that you readers always say what you think. So here's your chance. We'd really like your input for future printings and editions of this book — and ideas for future ...*For Dummies* titles as well. Tell us what you liked (and didn't like) about this book. How about the chapters you found most useful — or most funny? And since we know you're not a bit shy, what about the chapters you think can be improved? Just to show you how much we appreciate your input, we'll add you to our Dummies Database/Fan Club and keep you up to date on the latest ...*For Dummies* books, news, cartoons, calendars, and more! Please send your name, address, and phone number, as well as your comments, questions, and suggestions, to our very own ...For Dummies coordinator at the following address:

...*For Dummies* Coordinator
IDG Books Worldwide
3250 North Post Road, Suite 140
Indianapolis, IN 46226

(Yes, Virginia, there really is a ...*For Dummies* coordinator. We are not making this up.)

Please mention the name of this book in your comments.

Thanks for your input!

Don't forget to fill out the Reader Response Card in the back of this book and send it in!

About IDG Books Worldwide

Welcome to the world of IDG Books Worldwide.

IDG Books Worldwide, Inc., is a division of International Data Group, the world's largest publisher of computer-related information and the leading global provider of information services on information technology. IDG publishes over 194 computer publications in 62 countries. Forty million people read one or more IDG publications each month.

If you use personal computers, IDG Books is committed to publishing quality books that meet your needs. We rely on our extensive network of publications, including such leading periodicals as *Macworld, InfoWorld, PC World, Publish, Computerworld, Network World,* and *SunWorld,* to help us make informed and timely decisions in creating useful computer books that meet your needs.

Every IDG book strives to bring extra value and skill-building instruction to the reader. Our books are written by experts, with the backing of IDG periodicals, and with careful thought devoted to issues such as audience, interior design, use of icons, and illustrations. Our editorial staff is a careful mix of high-tech journalists and experienced book people. Our close contact with the makers of computer products helps ensure accuracy and thorough coverage. Our heavy use of personal computers at every step in production means we can deliver books in the most timely manner.

We are delivering books of high quality at competitive prices on topics customers want. At IDG, we believe in quality, and we have been delivering quality for over 25 years. You'll find no better book on a subject than an IDG book.

John Kilcullen
President and C.E.O.
IDG Books Worldwide, Inc.

IDG Books Worldwide, Inc. is a division of International Data Group. The officers are Patrick J. McGovern, Founder and Board Chairman; Walter Boyd, President. International Data Group's publications include: **ARGENTINA's** Computerworld Argentina, InfoWorld Argentina; **ASIA's** Computerworld Hong Kong, PC World Hong Kong, Computerworld Southeast Asia, PC World Singapore, Computerworld Malaysia, PC World Malaysia; **AUSTRALIA's** Computerworld Australia, Australian PC World, Australian Macworld, Network World, Reseller, IDG Sources; **AUSTRIA's** Computerwelt Oesterreich, PC Test; **BRAZIL's** Computerworld, Mundo IBM, Mundo Unix, PC World, Publish; **BULGARIA's** Computerworld Bulgaria, Ediworld, PC & Mac World Bulgaria; **CANADA's** Direct Access, Graduate Computerworld, InfoCanada, Network World Canada; **CHILE's** Computerworld, Informatica; **COLOMBIA's** Computerworld Colombia; **CZECH REPUBLIC's** Computerworld, Elektronika, PC World; **DENMARK's** CAD/CAM WORLD, Communications World, Computerworld Danmark, LOTUS World, Macintosh Produktkatalog, Macworld Danmark, PC World Danmark, PC World Produktguide, Windows World; **ECUADOR's** PC World; **EGYPT's** Computerworld (CW) Middle East, PC World Middle East; **FINLAND's** MikroPC, Tietoviikko, Tietoverkko; **FRANCE's** Distributique, GOLDEN MAC, InfoPC, Languages & Systems, Le Guide du Monde Informatique, Le Monde Informatique, Telecoms & Reseaux; **GERMANY's** Computerwoche, Computerwoche Focus, Computerwoche Extra, Computerwoche Karriere, Information Management, Macwelt, Netzwelt, PC Welt, PC Woche, Publish, Unit; **HUNGARY's** Alaplap, Computerworld SZT, PC World, ; **INDIA's** Computers & Communications; **ISRAEL's** Computerworld Israel, PC World Israel; **ITALY's** Computerworld Italia, Lotus Magazine, Macworld Italia, Networking Italia, PC World Italia; **JAPAN's** Computerworld Japan, Macworld Japan, SunWorld Japan, Windows World; **KENYA's** East African Computer News; **KOREA's** Computerworld Korea, Macworld Korea, PC World Korea; **MEXICO's** Compu Edicion, Compu Manufactura, Computacion/Punto de Venta, Computerworld Mexico, MacWorld, Mundo Unix, PC World, Windows; **THE NETHERLAND'S** Computer!Totaal, LAN Magazine, MacWorld; **NEW ZEALAND's** Computer Listings, Computerworld New Zealand, New Zealand PC World; **NIGERIA's** PC World Africa; **NORWAY's** Computerworld Norge, C/World, Lotusworld Norge, Macworld Norge, Networld, PC World Ekspress, PC World Norge, PC World's Product Guide, Publish World, Student Data, Unix World, Windowsworld, IDG Direct Response; **PANAMA's** PC World; **PERU's** Computerworld Peru, PC World; **PEOPLE'S REPUBLIC OF CHINA's** China Computerworld, PC World China, Electronics International, China Network World; **IDG HIGH TECH BEIJING's** New Product World; **IDG SHENZHEN's** Computerworld, PC World; **PHILIPPINES'** Computerworld, PC World; **POLAND's** Computerworld Poland, PC World/ Komputer; **PORTUGAL's** Cerebro/PC World, Correio Informatico/Computerworld, MacIn; **ROMANIA's** PC World; **RUSSIA's** Computerworld-Moscow, Mir-PC, Sety; **SLOVENIA's** Monitor Magazine; **SOUTH AFRICA's** Computing S.A.; **SPAIN's** Amiga World, Computerworld Espana, Communicaciones World, Macworld Espana, NeXTWORLD, PC World Espana, Publish, Sunworld; **SWEDEN's** Attack, ComputerSweden, Corporate Computing, Lokala Natverk/LAN, Lotus World, MAC&PC, Macworld, Mikrodatorn, PC World, Publishing & Design (CAP), Datalngenjoren, Maxi Data, Windows World; **SWITZERLAND's** Computerworld Schweiz, Macworld Schweiz, PC & Workstation; **TAIWAN's** Computerworld Taiwan, Global Computer Express, PC World Taiwan; **THAILAND's** Thai Computerworld; **TURKEY's** Computerworld Monitor, Macworld Turkiye, PC World Turkiye; **UNITED KINGDOM's** Lotus Magazine, Macworld, Sunworld; **UNITED STATES'** AmigaWorld, Cable in the Classroom, CD Review, CIO, Computerworld, Desktop Video World, DOS Resource Guide, Electronic News, Federal Computer Week, Federal Integrator, GamePro, IDG Books, InfoWorld, InfoWorld Direct, Laser Event, Macworld, Multimedia World, Network World, NeXTWORLD, PC Games, PC Letter, PC World Publish, Sumeria, SunWorld, SWATPro, Video Event; **VENEZUELA's** Computerworld Venezuela, MicroComputerworld Venezuela; **VIETNAM's** PC World Vietnam

About the Author

John Walkenbach has used spreadsheets for more than a decade, beginning with the old dinosaur of a program known as VisiCalc. He's a frequent contributor to magazines such as *PC World, PC/Computing, Windows,* and *InfoWorld* and author of several other spreadsheet books, including the *PC World Excel 5 for Windows Handbook.* He holds a Ph.D. in experimental psychology from the University of Montana and has worked as an instructor, programmer, consultant, and market research manager in the banking industry. When he's not writing about computers and software, he's probably playing around in his MIDI studio, working on his latest music-oriented shareware creation, or annoying his neighbors with weird synthetic sounds.

Contents at a Glance

Introduction

Greetings. You're holding in your hands one of a different breed of computer reference books — a book written for normal people (not computer geeks). The *Excel For Dummies Quick Reference* is for those of you who have no aspirations of becoming a spreadsheet wizard. Rather, you want to be able to do your job efficiently so you can move on to more important things — like having a life.

This Book: Who Needs It?

I wrote this book for the hundreds of thousands of beginning to intermediate Excel users who have better things to do with their time than wade through technical dribble just to figure out how to do something.

When I was asked to write this book, I visited several local bookstores to get an idea of what I would be competing with for shelf space. I found dozens of Excel books and Excel command reference guides. With a few exceptions, these books are dull, boring, too technical, and not much fun to read. An exception to this state of affairs is Greg Harvey's *Excel For Dummies*, Second Edition. Because of its light-hearted approach to teaching about computers and software, the ... *For Dummies* series is the most popular computer book series ever.

If you have absolutely no experience with Excel, *Excel For Dummies*, 2nd Edition is a better place to start. Actually, this book is designed to go hand in hand with Greg's book, so you might want to buy them both.

Why Another Excel Book?

Excel has always been the top-selling Windows spreadsheet. It has come a long way since it was first released in 1987, and most people who know about such things consider it to be the most powerful spreadsheet program available. Excel can be used at many different levels, and it's a safe bet that the majority of Excel users don't really have a clue as to what the program can really do when all the stops are pulled out. My goal is to open the door to some of the cool things that Excel can do — and do so in a way that doesn't put you to sleep.

On the one hand, Excel is very easy to use. I can spend 20 minutes with new users and have them doing semi-useful things by themselves after this initial session. But most Excel users eventually reach a head-scratching point in which they want to do something but can't figure out where the command is located. Or, they just can't seem to get a command to do what they think it *should* do.

Mousing Around

Some day, computers will be able to respond to your vocal commands. You could say something like, "Hey computer, run Excel and load that file I was working on Thursday afternoon. Then change the interest rate cell to 8.5 percent. Thanks, dude." Until that day arrives, you're going to have to give commands in a way that the computer can understand.

If you have used Excel for even a few minutes, you undoubtedly know that clicking the menu bar opens the door to a staggering number of commands by displaying drop-down menus. You can change how your numbers look, move stuff around, print your work, and even perform an analysis of variance if you're so moved.

The truth of the matter is that virtually no one actually needs or uses *all* the Excel commands. Most users get by just fine after they learn the basics. But if you stick to the basics, you run the risk of causing more work for yourself. For example, Excel has commands which automate things that may take you an hour to do manually. Saving 10 minutes here or a half hour there adds up over time. You'll have more time for fun things and can maybe even get out of the office at a reasonable hour — not to mention the fact that people will be amazed at how efficient you've become.

How the Commands Look

Because this reference guide is all about the Excel commands, we need to be on the same wavelength. In other words, you need to know where my head was at when I was writing all of this stuff and nonsense.

Most of this book consists of a discussion of Excel's commands. Here's an example using the File⇨Open command. As you may already know, this particular command brings up a dialog box that lets you choose a file to work on. When I talk about this command later on in the book, it'll appear in the heading as:

File⇨Open...

Notice that the *F* and the *O* are underlined. These are the *hot keys* that let you access the command from the keyboard. In this case, Alt+F,O will do the trick. Because the command name is followed by three dots (officially known as *ellipses*), you know right off the bat that issuing the command opens a dialog box.

In this book, the command name is followed by some icons (described later) that tell you at a glance some things about the command — how often you are likely to use it and how safe it is to use. The text for each command starts out with a brief English-language description of what it does. Then, I tell you why you would ever want (or need) to use this command and briefly explain how to use it. If there's anything else you should know about, you'll find it here. Finally, I refer you to other commands that may be of interest — one of them could be the one that you *really* want to use.

What the Little Pictures Mean

All the good computer books have little icons sprinkled liberally throughout their pages. These icons work great for visually oriented people and tell you in an instant a few key things about each command. If you're the type who grooves on icons, you'll appreciate that I've inserted plenty of them. Here's what the icons in this book mean:

 This icon flags commands that are used by almost all Excel users. It's probably worth your while to learn about this command.

 This icon flags commands that are generally not used by beginners, although you might have a use for them.

 This icon flags commands that are normally used only by advanced Excel users or for special purposes. These commands can be useful at times.

 This icon flags commands that are safe for your data.

 This icon flags commands that are generally safe in most circumstances unless you really don't follow instructions; then look out.

This command flags commands that are potentially dangerous to data but necessary in the scheme of things. Be careful when you use this command!

This icon flags a command that is available only if you have loaded a particular add-in file.

This icon flags commands that are available only when you're editing a chart.

This icon flags a command (or part of it) that is available as an icon on a toolbar.

This icon flags problem areas that can mess up your work if you're not on your toes.

This icon flags a way of using the command that may not be immediately obvious to the average bear.

This icon flags cross references to other areas of this book that might be of interest.

This icon flags material that tells you where to look in _Excel For Dummies, 2nd Edition_ for more information. If (for some unknown reason) you don't have _Excel For Dummies, 2nd Edition,_ don't even bother reading this stuff.

How You Can Use This Book

You can use this book in several ways.

- If you need to find out how to do something in Excel, look up the main menu command (they're listed in alphabetical order, not the order in which they appear on-screen) and browse through until you find something that looks relevant and then read it.

- If you don't have a clue as to the proper command to look up, head for the index and look at words that describe what you want to do. This search usually steers you to the command that you're looking for.

- If you need to find out why something isn't working the way you think it should, look up the command and read about it. I throw in all sorts of useful tips and techniques at no extra charge.

- If you find yourself with a spare hour or two while circling over LAX waiting to land, browse through it and read things that are interesting to you. If you find that nothing in this book passes that criterion, you're not alone. However, you just might discover something that you didn't know Excel could do — and it just might be what you need for a project you're working on.

- Keep it lying around on your desk. That way, people walking by will stop and make idle conversation while trying to get a look at the book without actually telling you they need the help! It's a good way to kill some time when you should be working.

How not to use this book: Whatever you do, don't read this book from cover to cover. Frankly, the plot stinks, the character development leaves much to be desired, and you will be disappointed with the ending. Although it's moderately entertaining, the book is not exactly what you would call a page-turner!

How I Organized This Book

This book is divided into five parts.

Part I: A Crash Course in Excel. This is a quick and dirty overview of Excel basics. I was tempted to leave this information out and simply refer you to *Excel For Dummies, 2nd Edition,* but I'm a nice guy.

Part II: The Excel Command Reference. Here's the heart of the book, as it were. It's an alphabetical listing of all the menu commands available when you're working in a worksheet or editing a chart — with just enough detail for most normal people.

Part III: The Dummies Guide to Excel's Toolbars. You can save yourself lots of time and effort by using the toolbars provided with Excel. But you need to know that the tools do and when to use them. Here's where you'll find the scoop on toolbar icons.

Part IV: The Dummies Guide to Excel's Worksheet Functions. All of those weird — but sometimes useful — functions are described here in language that you can understand.

Part V: The Dummies Guide to Excel's Keyboard Commands.
For one reason or another, some people prefer to use a mouse whenever possible. The fact is, you can often do things more quickly by using the keyboard. If doing things at warp speed appeals to you, read through this section to become familiar with the gajillion or so Excel keyboard commands at your disposal.

With that out of the way, let's move on to some actual substance.

Part 1:
A Crash Course in Excel

For those of you who haven't yet treated yourself to *Excel For Dummies*, 2nd Edition, here's the condensed version (but without the cartoons and jokes). You can read through this section to get a quick overview of Excel or use it to refresh those brain cells that have lost their charge. Be warned, however, that this section is by no means conclusive. In other words, I left out lots of tidbits that are explained more thoroughly in *Excel for Dummies*, 2nd Edition.

Basic Excel Knowledge

Excel is one of several spreadsheet programs that software vendors try to get you to buy. Other spreadsheets that you may have heard of include Lotus 1-2-3, Borland's Quattro Pro, and Computer Associates' SUPERNAL. Many others have come and gone over the years, but these are by far the most popular ones.

A *spreadsheet program* is essentially a highly interactive environment that lets you work with numbers and words in a large grid of cells. Excel, like all other spreadsheets, can also create graphs from numbers stored in a worksheet and work with database information stored in a record and field format.

Excel 5 uses workbook files with a CLOSE extension. A single workbook file can store as many sheets as fit into memory, and these sheets are stacked like the pages in a notebook. Sheets can be any of the following:

- Worksheets
- Chart sheets
- Excel 4.0 macro sheets
- Visual basic module sheets
- Dialog sheets

Most of the time, you will work with worksheets. Every Excel worksheet has 16,384 rows and 256 columns. *Rows* are numbered from 1 to 16384, and *columns* are labeled with letters. Column 1 is A, column 26 is Z, column 27 is AA, column 52 is AZ, column 53 is BA, and so on up to column 256 (which is IV).

The intersection of a row and column is called a *cell*. My calculator tells me that this works out to 4,194,304 cells — which should be enough for most people. Actually, you would run out of memory long before you even came *close* to using all the cells. Cells have addresses, which are based on the row and column that they are in. The upper left cell in a worksheet is called *A1*, and the cell way down at the bottom is called *IV256*. Cell *K9* (also known as the dog cell) is the intersection of the eleventh column and the ninth row.

A cell in Excel can hold a number, some text, a formula, or nothing at all. A formula is a special way to tell Excel to perform a calculation using information stored in other cells. For example, you can insert a formula that tells Excel to add up the values in the first 10 cells in column A, and display the result in the cell that has the formula. Formulas can use normal arithmetic operators such as + (plus), – (minus), * (multiply), and / (divide). They can also use special built-in functions that let you do powerful things without much effort on your part. For example, Excel has functions that add up a range of values, calculate square roots, compute loan payments, and even tell you the time of day. Excel's functions are listed in Part IV.

When you create a chart from numbers stored in a worksheet, you can put the chart directly on the worksheet or in special chart sheets in the workbook. When you're working with a chart, some of Excel's menus change.

The Active Cell and Ranges

In Excel, one of the cells in a worksheet is always the *active cell*. You can also select a group of cells by clicking and dragging the mouse over them. The *selected range* is usually a group of contiguous cells, but it doesn't have to be. If you hold down the Ctrl key while you click and drag the mouse, you can select more than one group of cells. Then, the commands you issue will work on all the selected cells. When you issue a command that does something to a cell or range, that something is done to the active cell or the selected range.

Navigational Techniques

With more than 4 million cells in a worksheet, you need ways to move to specific cells. Fortunately, Excel provides you with many techniques to move around through a worksheet. As always, you can use either your mouse or the keyboard on your navigational journeys. The navigational keys are covered in Part V.

The Excel Screen

The following figure shows a typical Excel screen, with some of the important parts pointed out. This terminology rears its ugly head throughout this book, so pay attention.

Filling up the Cells

A cell can hold a number, text, a formula, or nothing at all. If you want to put a number into the active cell, just start typing it and press Enter when you're done. Then, move to another cell and do it again.

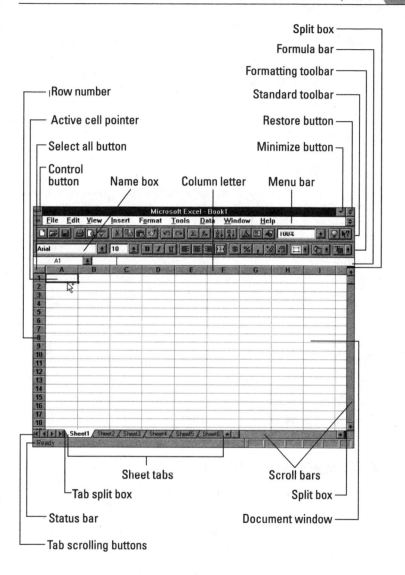

Split box
Formula bar
Formatting toolbar
Standard toolbar
Restore button
Minimize button

Row number
Active cell pointer
Select all button
Control button
Name box
Column letter
Menu bar

Microsoft Excel - Book1
File   Edit   View   Insert   Format   Tools   Data   Window   Help

Arial   10

A1

Sheet1 Sheet2 Sheet3 Sheet4 Sheet5 Sheet6

Ready

Sheet tabs
Tab split box
Status bar
Tab scrolling buttons

Scroll bars
Split box
Document window

To put text into the active cell, just start typing it and press Enter when you're done. You can put a lot of text in a cell — much more than you might think, given the width of a typical cell. If the cell to the right is empty, the text appears to "spill over" into it. If the neighboring cell is not empty, the text appears to get cut off if it's wider than the column (it's all there, it just doesn't show).

Entering formulas is another story. Usually, formulas refer to other cells and use their values. Here's a simple formula:

```
=(A1+A2)/2
```

This formula adds the values in cells A1 and A2 and divides the result by 2. Cells A1 and A2 can hold either numbers or other formulas. If either of these cells has a label (text), Excel interprets it as zero. Whenever either cell A1 or A2 changes, the formula displays a new answer.

Charts and Drawings

You can produce some awesome charts with Excel, with minimal effort. Charts use numbers stored in a worksheet, and if any of the numbers change, the chart redraws automatically to reflect those changes. Excel offers a staggering number of chart types, and you can waste hours customizing charts to give them just the right look.

Besides charts, you can create simple drawings directly on a worksheet. For example, you can create flow diagrams, add arrows and lines, draw a circle around a cell, and even bring in full-color clip art files.

Macros and Dialog Boxes

Advanced users appreciate some of the other capabilities of Excel. It has two macro languages built in to automate procedures, and it's fairly easy to create custom dialog boxes. Since these topics are beyond the interest level of my target reader for this book, that's all I'm going to say.

Giving Commands to Excel

Excel has many commands that you use to do the things that spreadsheet users do. Here's a typical Excel command: File⇨Open. This command is used to read a workbook file into Excel so that you can work on it.

You can invoke this command in several different ways.

- Click on the File menu with the mouse and then click on the Open command.
- Press Alt+F (for File) and then O (for Open).

- Press Alt or the F10 key to activate the menu bar; then use the arrow keys to move to the File menu. Press Enter and use the arrow keys to move to the Open command. Press Enter again to issue the command.

- Click on the icon on the Standard toolbar that looks like a file folder opening up.

- Press Ctrl+F12 (or Alt+Ctrl+F2 if your keyboard lacks an F12 function key).

All these techniques lead to the end result of the File Open dialog box, which you use to tell Excel which file you want to open. After the dialog box appears, you can use your mouse or keyboard to carry on the dialogue and tell Excel what you're trying to do.

Although having all these command-issuing options available may seem a bit confusing, you don't have to learn them all. Most people simply learn one method and stick to it. Also, not all commands have so many options. Since the File⇨Open command is used so frequently, Excel designers went overboard and came up with several ways to do it.

Most commands lead to a dialog box, but some commands do their thing immediately with no additional work required on your part. You can tell the commands that lead to a dialog box because they are followed by ellipses (...) in the drop-down menu.

There is yet another way to issue commands in Excel. Right-clicking objects, an individual cell, or a selected range of cells displays a shortcut menu that lists common commands that are appropriate to the selection. The figure shows the shortcut menu that appears when you right-click after selecting a range of cells.

Working with Dialog Boxes

Excel, like virtually every other Windows application, is big on dialog boxes. A *dialog box* is a small window that pops up in response to most of the commands that you issue. This window is displayed right on top of what you're doing — a sure sign that you must make some type of response to the dialog box before you can do anything else.

The figure shows a typical Excel dialog box. This particular dialog box is displayed when you select the File⇨Page Setup command. I chose this for an example because it contains many (but not all) of the types of dialog box controls that you're likely to encounter.

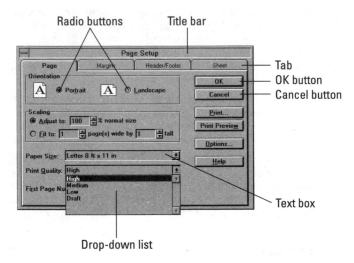

Dialog Box Parts

Here's a fairly exhaustive list of the various controls and other parts you will be up against in the world of dialog boxes.

Dialog Box Part (s)	Operation
Title bar	Click and drag the title bar to move the dialog box to a different part of the screen if it's covering up something you want to see.

Dialog Box Part(s)	*Operation*
Tab	Click on a tab to change the dialog box to display a whole new set of controls.
Radio buttons	Round buttons, usually enclosed in a group box. Only one radio button in a group can be "on" at a time. When you click on a radio button, the others in the group are turned off — just like an old-fashioned car radio.
Drop-down list	A list of things you can choose from. These lists have a small downward-pointing arrow. Click on the arrow to drop the list down.
Text box	A box in which you enter something — a number or text.
Check box	A square box that you can click on to turn the option on or off.
List box	A box that shows several choices. It usually has a vertical scroll bar that you can click on to show more items in the list.
OK button	The button to click on when you've made your dialog box selections and want to get on with it.
Cancel button	The button to click on if you change your mind. None of the changes you made to the dialog box will take effect.
Help button	The button to click on to display the relevant section from Excel's on-line help system.
Button	A dialog box button you choose in order to do something else. If the text on the button has three dots after it, clicking on it brings up another dialog box.

Navigating Through Dialog Boxes

You can work with a dialog box using your mouse or the keyboard. The choice is yours.

If you use a mouse, simply position the mouse pointer on the option you want to work with and click. The exact procedure varies with the type of control, but the good news is that all Windows programs work the same way. If you learn to use Excel dialog boxes, you'll have a head start when you try to learn another Windows program. And if you already use other Windows programs, you'll feel right at home with Excel's dialog boxes.

Notice that the various parts of a dialog box have text with a single underlined letter. You can use the Alt key along with this letter to jump to that particular component. For example, the Page Setup dialog box has a text box that's preceded by text that reads, First Page Number. Because the r is underlined, pressing Alt+R puts the cursor in the text box so you can type your option. Besides using Alt key combinations, you can use Tab and Shift+Tab to cycle through all of the controls in a dialog box.

Mousing Around with Toolbars

One of the greatest time-saving features in Excel is its toolbars. Excel comes with 13 toolbars, each of which has a bunch of icons that provide shortcuts for commonly used commands and procedures. For example, there's an icon to left-align the contents of a cell or range. This is *much* faster than issuing the Format⇨Cells command, choosing the Alignment tab, and then selecting the Left option in the dialog box. To make a long story short, it's well worth your effort to learn about Excel's toolbars. Your opportunity to do so comes up in Part III.

Actually Doing Things with Excel

The process of using Excel involves entering data and formulas into cells, manipulating the data in various ways using the menu commands and dialog boxes, and then printing the results on paper for the rest of the world to enjoy. And if you're smart, you will take advantage of the toolbar icons, shortcut keys, and shortcut menus to make the process even easier. Not coincidentally, all these things are covered in the rest of this book.

Part II:
Excel Command Reference

OK folks, here's the good stuff. The reason you laid your hard-earned money (or, hopefully, your company's money) on the counter for this information-packed little book.

The following pages explain every single Excel command that you can possibly give. Well, actually, I left some out. This chapter covers every command available when you're working with a worksheet or a chart. It does *not* cover the commands available only in Visual Basic modules, dialog box sheets, or XLM macro sheets. Only advanced users need these commands, and including them in this book would only add more confusion.

I'll be the first to admit that I provide the best explanations for the most commonly used commands — but that's probably why you chose this book in the first place, right? But if you're ever held at gunpoint and ordered to insert an OLE object into a worksheet, you can rest assured that you can find out what it's all about by venturing no farther than the book you now hold in your hand.

If you find that some of the commands listed here don't show up on your menu, that's because the command is enabled by loading an add-in file. All these add-in commands are identified by an icon. To make the command available, use the Tools➪Add-Ins command and choose the appropriate add-in from the displayed list. If you cannot find the add-in that you need, you must run Excel's Setup program and tell it that you want to install the particular add-in.

Data Menu Commands

The Data menu is where it's happening when you're working with a *worksheet database* — an organized collection of information arranged by records (rows) and fields (columns). It also houses the commands to sort cells and ranges, create and manipulate outlines, and do lots of other things that are best described as advanced.

Data⇨_Consolidate..._

Lets you combine corresponding cells from different ranges or different worksheets. It can do so "intelligently" by matching row and column titles. If you're in charge of your company's budget and need to consolidate individual departmental budgets into a master corporate budget, this command can save you hours of manual labor. But the command's usefulness extends beyond budgeting and is handy for all sorts of consolidation chores.

How you use it

First, make sure all the worksheets to be consolidated (the "source" documents) are available and that the ranges to be consolidated are all set up identically (or at least use the same row and column headers). Issue the Data⇨Consolidate command and fill in the dialog box, specifying the references in each worksheet to the list.

More stuff

Besides summing the corresponding values, you can choose from a variety of other mathematical operations in the Function drop-down list in the Consolidate dialog box.

If you check the box labeled Create links to Source data, Excel creates formulas that use external references. This can be very confusing if you don't know what you're doing, but it makes the consolidation happen automatically if any of the data in the worksheets you're consolidating get changed.

Data⇨Filter⇨Advanced Filter...

This command lets you specify more filtering criteria than is possible using the Data⇨Filter⇨AutoFilter command. In the vast majority of cases, simple autofiltering does the job.

How you use it

Before you can use this command you need to set up a criteria range somewhere in your worksheet. This consists of at least two rows, with field names in the first row and the criteria listed below. For example, if you want to select records in the database that have the word *Gopher* in the Animal field, the criterion range would consist of two cells: Animal and Gopher directly below it. Once you get the criteria range set up, move the cell pointer anywhere within the database and choose Data⇨Filter⇨Advanced Filter. The dialog box lets you specify whether to filter the list in place or copy the results elsewhere. If you do the filtering in place, Excel hides all the rows that don't qualify. If you copy the results elsewhere, it extracts the qualifying records and copies them to the new location.

More stuff

The criteria range doesn't have to include all the fields from the database. In fact, it can consist of as few as one field.

Data⇨Filter⇨AutoFilter, Data⇨Filter⇨Show All

Data⇨Filter⇨AutoFilter

Converts column titles into pull-down lists that allow you to more easily display only the data you want. This command is intended for information set up as a worksheet database.

How you use it

Move the active cell pointer anywhere in the database table and choose the Data⇨Filter⇨AutoFilter command. Excel checks out your worksheet and converts the labels at the top into drop-down list boxes. Choose the value that you want to display, and Excel hides all the rows that don't qualify.

More stuff

You can filter your data by any number of columns. If you want to get fancy, choose the option called (Custom...). The dialog box that appears lets you further specify your criteria. For example, you could choose to show only the rows in which the Month is Jan or Feb. To return things to normal, choose this command again, and Excel changes the column headers back to normal text.

Data⇨_Filter_⇨_Advanced Filter

Data⇨_Filter_⇨_Show All_

This command is available only if you filtered your data using the _Data_⇨_Filter_⇨_AutoFilter_ command or the _Data_⇨_Filter_⇨_Advanced Filter command. It's just a shortcut way to display all the rows that are hidden as a result of filtering your data.

How you use it

Just choose the command, and all hidden rows reappear as if by magic. The headers don't change back to normal. Choose _Data_⇨_Filter_⇨_AutoFilter_ again to turn off autofiltering.

Data⇨_Filter_⇨_AutoFilter, _Data_⇨_Filter_⇨_Advanced Filter

Data⇨_Form_...

Displays a handy form that simplifies entering data into an Excel database, browsing through a database, or locating or deleting records that meet simple criteria. Many people find that doing routine database entry using a form is easier than entering the stuff directly into the worksheet. Using this command is also a handy way to view database records.

How you use it

First, move the active cell pointer anywhere within the database. Then, when you issue the _Data_⇨_Form_ command, Excel displays a form that shows all your database fields, listed vertically. You can use the vertical scroll bar to scroll though the records.

More stuff

The dialog box that pops up when you choose the Data⤳Form command has lots of buttons on it. You can add a new record, delete the displayed record, and enter simple search criteria to limit the records displayed.

Data⤳Get External Data...

Starts up Query so that you can bring in selected data from an external database file. Query is a separate program that works with database files. The results of a query are stored in an Excel worksheet.

How you use it

After you choose this command, Query is started up (but Excel continues running). Use the commands in Query to identify the external database you want to work with and specify the criteria for retrieving records.

More stuff

This command is available only when the Query add-in is installed.

Data⤳Group and Outline⤳ Auto Outline

Creates an outline from a range of data that's set up appropriately. If your worksheet has hierarchical information — such as budget categories, with subcategories — it may be useful to be able to collapse the categories to show only a desired level. This command also works horizontally, so that you can collapse months into quarterly subtotals, for example.

How you use it

Select the range that you want to outline, and choose Data⇨Group and Outline⇨Auto Outline. Excel creates the outline and displays all the outline thingamajigs in the borders. This notation lets you expand and collapse the outline to see various levels of detail.

Not all spreadsheets are appropriate for outlines, and you usually need to do some upfront preparation to get the type of results you want.

Data⇨Group and Outline⇨ Clear Outline

Clears an existing outline and returns things to normal.

How you use it

Move the active cell point anywhere within an outlined range and choose Data⇨Group and Outline⇨Clear Outline. The outline disappears before you can say, "Where'd the buttons go?" This command doesn't remove any cells, just the outline structure.

More stuff

If you just want to get rid of the outline symbol display to keep it from taking up screen space (and keep the outline), use the Tools⇨Options command (View tab) and uncheck the Outline Symbols check box under Window Options.

Data⇨Group and Outline⇨Group...

Creates a group in an outline from selected rows or columns.

How you use it

Select the rows or columns that you want to group; then issue the
Data⇨Group and Outline⇨Group command.

Data⇨Group and Outline⇨ Hide Detail

Collapses an outline to hide all the details.

How you use it

Start by selecting the entire outlined range. Issue the command,
and the detail vanishes.

Data⇨Group and Outline⇨Show Detail

Data⇨Group and Outline⇨ Settings...

Creates an outline from a selected range. This command uses the
manual approach, and you may want to use the Data⇨Group and
Outline⇨Auto Outline command instead.

How you use it

Select the range to be outlined and choose Data⇨Group and
Outline⇨Settings. Complete the dialog box.

More stuff

You can also use this command to apply cell formatting to an
existing outline. Just select the outline, choose this command,
and click on Apply Styles.

Data⇨Group and Outline⇨Auto Outline

Data⇨Group and Outline⇨ Show Detail

Shows all the detail in an outline.

How you use it

Select the entire outlined range and issue the command. The outline expands to show everything.

Data⇨Group and Outline⇨Hide Detail

Data⇨Group and Outline⇨ Ungroup...

Ungroups a group in an outline.

How you use it

Select the rows or columns and issue the command.

Data⇨Pivot Table Field...

Lets you change various aspects of a field when you are working with a pivot table. For example, you can change the field name displayed or choose a different way of summarizing the field.

How you use it

After you create a pivot table, select a field and choose Data⇨Pivot Table Field. Excel displays a dialog box that lets you set the options.

More stuff

You can also double-click on the field name to get to the dialog box or use the Pivot Table tool on the toolbar.

Data ⇨ Pivot Table...

Converts a database into an interactive multidimensional pivot table. If your data are in a pivot table, you can drag the field names around to change the way the data are displayed.

How you use it

Issue the Data ⇨ Pivot Table command, and Excel's PivotTable Wizard kicks in. You can select a worksheet database or an external database and consolidate multiple tables into a single pivot table.

More stuff

Not all databases are appropriate for pivot tables.

Data ⇨ Refresh Data

Reruns a previously executed database query. This command is relevant only if you use data from an external database.

How you use it

After executing a query with the Data ⇨ Get External Data command, move the cell pointer anywhere within the results table and issue this command. Excel starts Query and refreshes the results.

More stuff

This command is available only when the active cell is part of a Query results table or a pivot table that has been generated using external data.

Data⇨Get External Data, Data⇨Pivot Table

Data⇨Sort...

Rearranges a range of cells into ascending or descending order, using one or more rows or columns as a sorting key. There are lots of reasons why you may want to sort data: to make finding things easier, to present results from best to worst, to alphabetize a list, to sort entries by date, and so on.

How you use it

First, move the cell pointer anywhere within the range that you want to sort. Issue the Data⇨Sort command. In the Sort dialog box, choose the column on which you want to sort and select either Ascending or Descending. If the range has a header row, Excel displays these titles (rather than column letters) in the Sort by drop-down list. Choose as many as three sort keys.

More stuff

Sorting rows is most common, but if you want to sort columns, click on the Options button and choose Sort Left to Right.

See *Excel For Dummies*, 2nd Edition, Chapter 8 for more about sorting.

Data⇨Subtotals...

Inserts formulas within a database to calculate subtotals.

How you use it

Start with a database and sort it by the field that you want to compute subtotals. For example, if you have an employee database with fields called Location and Salary, you might want to compute total salaries for each location. In this case, sort by Location. Make sure that the active cell pointer is somewhere in the database and issue the Data⇨Subtotals command. The dialog box that you get is fairly straightforward. Continuing with the employee example, complete the dialog box so that it says: at each change in Location use function SUM and add subtotal to Salary. Click on OK, and Excel goes to work and creates formulas in a flash.

More stuff

Excel also creates an outline, so you can hide the detail and just show the subtotal rows. If you don't care to deal with the outline, use the Data⇨Group and Outline⇨Clear Outline command. To remove the subtotals, issue the command again and click on the Remove All button. Everything returns to normal.

Data⇨Table...

Creates a table that shows how specific cells in your worksheet change when another cell (or cells) is changed. Some worksheets are set up with formulas that allow you to ask "what if" questions. For example, "What if we raise prices by 5 percent?" or "What if I get fired next week?" This command can summarize the results of a bunch of what-if scenarios in the form of a nicely formatted table.

How you use it

This is a pretty advanced command, and I would need to write several pages to do it justice. Frankly, using Excel's Scenario Manager is much better way to go.

Tools⇨Scenarios

Data⇨Text to Columns...

Breaks text into component parts in separate columns. This command is useful if you copy information from another program and it shows up in a single column.

How you use it

Select the cells in a single column that holds the text and choose Data⇨Text to Columns. Excel displays a three-part "wizard" that guides you through the steps. Most of the time, this command works without a hitch.

Edit Menu Commands

In computer lingo, changing something is usually called editing. Excel's Edit menu gives you lots of options when you need to make changes to your worksheet, rearrange things, copy things, and so on.

Edit⇨Clear⇨All

Clears everything from a cell or range.

How you use it

Select the cell or range that you want to clear and then choose Edit⇨Clear⇨All. It's outta here.

More stuff

Don't confuse this with the Edit⇨Delete command, which not only clears the cells but also removes them (and shifts the other cells around to accommodate their removal).

A common error people make is using the spacebar to "delete" the contents of a cell. Actually, they place a character in the cell — which happens to be invisible, so that it looks as if the cell is empty. The fact is that using the spacebar to delete can cause you major problems that are difficult to diagnose. So take my advice and don't erase cells with the spacebar. Thanks.

Edit⇨Delete

Edit⇨Clear⇨Contents

Clears only the contents from a cell or range.

How you use it

Select the cell or range that you want to clear and then choose Edit⇨Clear⇨Contents. The cell contents are gone, but any formatting or cell notes linger on.

You can also erase the contents of cells by pressing the Delete key. Yet another way is to use the fill handle. Select the range that you want to erase and then drag the fill handle up or left with your mouse. The cells that you drag over will have a shaded pattern on them. Release the mouse button, and the contents of all the shaded cells are erased (formats remain, however).

Edit⇨Clear⇨Formats

Clears only the formats from a cell or range.

How you use it

Select the cell or range that you want to clear and then choose Edit⇨Clear⇨Formats. Any formatting that you applied is gone (but the cell contents remain).

Edit⇨Clear⇨Notes

Clears any cell notes from a cell or range.

How you use it

Select the cell or range that you want to clear and then choose Edit⇨Clear⇨Notes. If the selection contained any cells with cell notes, the notes disappear.

Edit⇨Copy

Copies whatever is selected to the Windows Clipboard. It can then be pasted into another location in an Excel worksheet or even into another Windows application. This command is commonly used, and you won't get too far without it.

How you use it

First, select the cell or range that you want to copy. Choose the Edit⇨Copy command. Excel displays a moving "marquee" around the selection and a message at the bottom of the screen asking you to choose the destination and press Enter or choose Paste. If you move to a new location and press Enter, Excel pastes the copied cells to the new cell pointer position. If you move to a new location and choose Edit⇨Paste, Excel pastes the copied cells there and *leaves them on the Clipboard* so you can paste them somewhere else.

If you want to make multiple copies of a cell or range, use Edit⇨Copy followed by Edit⇨Paste (multiple times). Pressing Enter removes the stuff from the Clipboard.

If you attempt to copy to a location that already contains information, Excel overwrites it without warning.

More stuff

You can also use this command to copy text from the formula bar. If you're creating a formula that's similar to one that already exists, you can steal the relevant part of the formula from the existing formula by copying it. Then, use Edit⇨Paste at the appropriate place in the formula you're creating.

If you're copying something to neighboring cells, you might prefer to copy simply by dragging the AutoFill handle on the cell or range that you're copying.

If you're simply copying from one cell to the cell below, use Ctrl+' to copy the formula from the cell above or Ctrl+Shift+' to copy the value from the cell above. Also, if you select a range before you enter a formula, you can use Ctrl+Enter to put the formula into all cells in the selection in one fell swoop (saving you from copying it later).

Ctrl+C is a shortcut for Edit⇨Copy.

Edit⇨Fill⇨Down, Edit⇨Fill⇨Up, Edit⇨Fill⇨Left, Edit⇨Fill Right

Edit⇨Copy Picture...

Copies an image of the selection to the Clipboard, so that you can use it as a graphic. This command might be handy if you want to include part of your worksheet in a graphics program or if you need to show part of an Excel worksheet in a training manual produced with a word processor. **Note:** This command appears only if you hold down the Shift key while you choose the Edit command.

How you use it

Select a cell or cells, press Shift, and then choose Edit⇨Copy Picture. Excel responds with a dialog box in which you can choose some options. Usually, the default settings are fine. Choose OK to copy a pictorial representation of the selection to the Clipboard.

Edit⇨Paste Picture, Edit⇨Paste Picture Link

Edit⇨Cut

Cuts (i.e., deletes) whatever is selected and puts it on the Windows Clipboard. It can then be pasted into another location in an Excel worksheet or into another Windows application. This is the way to move a cell or range from one place to another.

How you use it

First, select the cell or range that you want to cut. Choose the Edit⇨Cut command. Excel displays a moving "marquee" around the selection and a message at the bottom of the screen asking you to choose the destination and press Enter or choose Paste. Move the cell cursor to the new location and press Enter, and Excel pastes the cut cells to the new cell pointer position.

If you move to a new location and choose Edit⇨Paste, Excel pastes the copied cells there but *does not* leave them on the Clipboard (so you can't paste them again somewhere else). Note that this differs from how pasting works when you copy stuff with the Edit⇨Copy command.

Be careful that you don't confuse this with Edit⇨Delete or Edit⇨Clear — both of which remove stuff from cells, not move it to the Clipboard.

If you attempt to move a cell or range to a location that already contains information, Excel will overwrite it without warning.

More stuff

Ctrl+X is a shortcut for Edit⇨Cut.

Edit⇨Copy, Edit⇨Paste, Edit⇨Delete, Edit⇨Clear

Edit⇨Delete...

Removes entire rows or columns. You can also use it to get rid of a cell or range of cells — but it shifts everything else around to fill up the blanks.

How you use it

Select the cell, range, row(s), or column(s) you want to get rid of and then choose the Edit⇨Delete command. If the selection is a cell or range, Excel displays a dialog box that asks you how you want to shift the other cells around to fill up the hole. Otherwise, it zaps the selection. If you delete rows, it shifts all the other rows up. If you delete columns, it shifts the other columns to the left.

More stuff

Be careful when you use this command on a single cell or a range. Shifting cells around can cause other parts of your worksheet to get messed up — and you may not realize it until later.

Edit⇨Clear, Edit⇨Cut

Edit⇨Delete Sheet

Permanently deletes one or more sheets in a workbook.

How you use it

Activate the sheet you want to delete and then choose this command. To delete more than one sheet, hold down Ctrl while you click on the tabs of the sheets you want to erase. Then, choose this command to delete them all.

More stuff

Be careful with this one. If you have formulas that use values in a sheet that you delete, the formulas are no longer valid.

This operation can't be reversed with the Edit⇨Undo command.

Edit⇨Fill⇨Across Worksheets...

Copies a cell or range to other worksheets in a workbook.

How you use it

Select the cell or range you want to copy; then hold down Ctrl while you click on the tabs of the sheets you want to copy to. Choose the command and respond to Excel's dialog box.

This command will overwrite existing information with no warning.

Edit⇨Copy

Edit⇨Fill⇨Down

Copies the first cell (or top row of cells) in a range to all the other cells below it in the selection. This is one way to quickly copy a cell or range to an adjacent cell or range. You might find that Excel's AutoFill feature is more efficient for this task.

How you use it

Start your selection at the cell or single-row range you want to copy and then extend the selection down to include all the cells you want to copy it to. Choose Edit⇨Fill⇨Down, and Excel copies the cell or range.

Edit⇨Copy

Edit⇨Fill⇨Justify

Rearranges a single-column range of cells that contains text so that it fits into a specified number of columns. If you use large blocks of text in your worksheet to provide instructions or explanatory information, "re-wrapping" the text to make it wider or narrower is easier with this command. It is much easier than editing the cells individually.

How you use it

Select the single-column range of text; then increase the selection to include additional columns that represent how wide you want the text to be. Choose Edit⇨Fill⇨Justify, and Excel redistributes the text to fit in the range you selected. To make text narrower, you need to select additional rows to hold the text. If the text doesn't fit in the range you select, Excel will ask you if it's okay to go outside of the range. If you respond in the affirmative, anything that may be outside of the range will be wiped out.

More stuff

This command doesn't work with cells that contain values or formulas. You can use a blank cell to simulate a new paragraph.

Edit⇨Fill⇨Left

Copies the rightmost cell (or right column of cells) in a range to all the other cells to the left of the selection. This command is one way to copy a cell or range to an adjacent cell or range quickly. You might find that Excel's AutoFill feature is more efficient for this task.

How you use it

Start your selection at the cell or single-column range you want to copy and then extend the selection to the left to include all the cells you want to copy it to. Choose Edit⇨Fill⇨Left, and Excel copies the cell or range.

This command will overwrite existing information with no warning.

Edit⇨Copy

Edit⇨Fill⇨Right

Copies the first cell (or left column of cells) in a range to all the other cells to the right of the selection. This command is one way to copy a cell or range to an adjacent cell or range quickly. You might find that Excel's AutoFill feature is more efficient for this task.

How you use it

Start your selection at the cell or single-column range you want to copy and then extend the selection to the right to include all the cells you want to copy it to. Choose Edit⇨Fill⇨Right, and Excel copies the cell or range.

This command will overwrite existing information with no warning.

Edit⇨Copy

Edit⇨Fill⇨Series...

Fills up a range with numbers, dates, times, or even words such as month or day names very quickly.

How you use it

Lots of options are available in the Series dialog box. Click on the Help button for more information.

The AutoFill feature is a faster way of accomplishing the same thing. Drag the AutoFill handle using the right mouse button to get a shortcut menu of fill options.

This command will overwrite existing information with no warning.

Edit⇨Copy

Edit⇨Fill⇨Up

Copies the last cell (or bottom row of cells) in a range to all the other cells above it in the selection. This is one way to copy a cell or range to an adjacent cell or range quickly. You might find that Excel's AutoFill feature is more efficient for this task.

How you use it

Start your selection at the cell or single-row range you want to copy and then extend the selection up to include all the cells you want to copy it to. Choose Edit⇨Fill⇨Up, and Excel copies the cell or range.

This command will overwrite existing information with no warning.

Edit⇨Copy

Edit⇨Find...

Searches through the worksheet for a specific string or number. This command is a fast way to locate something you're looking for without spending all you time at the keyboard.

How you use it

First, select the range you want to search. If you don't select a range, Excel looks in the entire active worksheet. Choose Edit⇨Find and complete the dialog box Excel displays. Click on OK to find the first occurrence. Then, you can use the F7 key to find the next one (or Shift+F7 to find the previous one).

Edit⇨Replace

Edit ⇨ Go To...

Lets you specify a cell or named cell or range to select. This command is a fast way to select a named range or move to a specific place in your worksheet.

How you use it

Select Edit⇨GoTo and then choose the named range you want. You can also enter a cell or range reference directly.

More stuff

The F5 key is a shortcut for this command.

Edit ⇨ Links...

Lets you update or change links to other worksheets or files (using OLE or DDE). If your workbook has references to other workbooks, this command forces them to be updated. For example, a formula might contain a link to another workbook on a network server. If the linked worksheet gets changed by someone, you can update the references with the Edit⇨Links command.

How you use it

Choose Edit⇨Links and then select the appropriate option. If you want to change the worksheet that you're linking to, use the Change button and select a new file. If you simply want to update the links, use the Update button.

Make sure that you know what you're doing. If you specify an incorrect file, you could mess up your formulas.

More stuff

This command is not available if your workbook doesn't contain any links.

Edit⇨Move or Copy Sheet

Moves or copies a sheet to another workbook or to another location in the same workbook.

How you use it

Select the sheet(s) you want to copy or move; then choose Edit⇨Move or Copy Sheet. Excel responds with a dialog box. Choose the workbook you want to move or copy to (it must be open) and the location for the new arrivals. If you want to copy it, check the Create a Copy check box.

More stuff

You can also move a sheet simply by dragging its tab. You can drag it to another location in the same workbook or even to a different workbook.

Edit⇨Object...

Allows you to edit an OLE object inserted into your workbook. OLE stands for Object Linking and Embedding, and an OLE object can be a drawing, a document, or many other types of things.

How you use it

Before you can edit an object, you must insert it by using the Insert⇨Object command.

More stuff

If the object is an OLE 2 object, the editing occurs directly in the document. Otherwise, you are switched to the application that originally created the document.

Insert⇨Object

Edit⇨Paste

Copies whatever is on the Windows Clipboard into your work-book. This is the second step in copy/paste or cut/paste operations.

How you use it

Once the cell or range is in the Clipboard (using the Edit⇨Copy or Edit⇨Cut commands), move the cell pointer to where you want to paste it and choose Edit⇨Paste.

If the cells in the paste area are not empty, Excel will overwrite them without warning.

More stuff

If you used the Edit⇨Copy command to put the stuff in the Clipboard, you can paste multiple copies of the Clipboard contents throughout your worksheet. This command also works with graphic objects.

Edit⇨Copy, Edit⇨Cut, Edit⇨Paste Special

Edit⇨Paste Picture

Pastes the Clipboard contents as a picture. **Note:** This command appears only if you hold down the Shift key while you choose the Edit menu.

How you use it

Select a range of cells and use Edit➪Copy or Edit➪Copy Picture to copy them to the Clipboard. Then, use Edit➪Paste Picture to paste a picture of the cells elsewhere.

Edit➪Copy, Edit➪Copy Picture, Edit➪Paste Picture Link

Edit➪_Paste Picture Link_

Pastes the Clipboard contents as a picture and creates a link to the original data. This command is useful if you need to show a picture of information that may change. **Note:** This command appears only if you hold down the Shift key while you choose the Edit menu.

How you use it

After copying the information to the Clipboard, press Shift and choose Edit➪Paste Picture Link. Excel creates a linked picture.

More stuff

The picture that you paste can be from Excel or any other application.

Edit➪Copy, Edit➪Copy Picture, Edit➪Paste Picture

Edit➪_Paste Special..._

Lets you paste only "part" of a copied selection — or lets you paste a selection in special ways. Use this command when you want to copy only values (no formats), only formats (no values), or notes from a cell or range to another cell or range. When you are copying, it also lets you transpose a range — turn a vertical range into a horizontal range. Finally, it lets you perform a mathematical operation on data that were already copied.

How you use it

Start by copying the cell or range. Then, move the cell pointer to a new position (or keep it where it is if you want to replace what you are copying). Choose Edit⇨Paste Special and select the options you want.

This command is useful if you want to change a range of cells by a certain amount and don't want to bother with formulas. For example, to multiply all cells in a range by 1.05 (which effectively increases each of them by 5 percent), put 1.05 in a cell and copy it to the Clipboard with the Edit⇨Copy command. Then, select the range that you want to modify and choose the Edit⇨Paste Special command. Select the Multiply option and choose OK. All the entries in the range are multiplied by 1.05.

More stuff

If the Clipboard contains data copied from another Windows application, Excel gives you the opportunity to do other things with the data when you choose Edit⇨Paste Special. For example, you can paste a link to a word processing document.

Edit⇨Copy, Edit⇨Paste

Edit⇨Redo (u) [Action]

Reverses the effects of Edit⇨Undo. In other words, it undoes an undo. Use this command if you didn't really want to undo an action.

More stuff

This command appears only after you choose Edit⇨Undo, and it lists the actual undo operation that will be undone.

Edit⇨Undo

Edit⇨Repeat [Action]

 Repeats the last thing you did. It's a great time-saver that can eliminate many a trip to the menu when you're doing boring, repetitious things.

How you use it

Do something and then choose Edit⇨Repeat to do it again.

More stuff

The F4 key is a shortcut for this.

 Most, but not all, actions are repeatable. The actual command name changes to tell you what will be repeated when you issue the command. Make sure it's really what you want. If the action can't be repeated, the command will read, Can't Repeat.

Edit⇨Replace...

Replaces a specific text string or a number in a worksheet with another text string or number. This command is a quick way to make lots of changes. For example, if your company changes its name from NerdCom to GeekCorp, you can use this command to change every occurrence of the old name to the new name.

How you use it

First, select the range you want to search. If you don't select a range, Excel looks in the entire active worksheet. Choose Edit⇨Replace and complete the dialog box Excel displays. Use the buttons on the right side of the dialog box to find additional matches or to replace everything.

 Edit⇨Find

Edit⇨Undo [Action]

Reverses the effect of the last thing you did. This command can be a real life-saver when you discover that the command you just issued didn't do what you thought it would do. You can also use this command to change something temporarily to see what happens (it is a sort of "what-if"). After checking out the results, use Edit⇨Undo to get things back to the way they used to be.

How you use it

Immediately after you discover your boo-boo (and before you do anything else), choose Edit⇨Undo to restore your worksheet to its condition before the faux pas. The actual command name reflects what it undoes. For example, after you sort a range, the command reads Undo Sort.

It's vitally important that you don't do anything between the time that you make your mistake and the time that you choose Edit⇨Undo. You should get in the habit of looking at what you did before moving on to the next step.

More stuff

Sometimes, what you are doing requires lots of memory and cannot be "undone." Excel always warns you in advance if you're performing an action that you won't be able to undo. In such a case, you should save your worksheet first so that you can undo the command by retrieving the saved version of your file.

Ctrl+Z is a shortcut for Edit⇨Undo. Think of it as "zapping" your mistakes away.

The "ultimate" undo is to save your file before you do something you are unsure about. Then, if it doesn't work, you can retrieve your saved file.

Edit⇨Redo (u), File⇨Save

File Menu Commands

Care to take a guess what the commands in this menu deal with? Besides loading and saving files, you'll also find the commands that deal with *printing*. This is pretty strange, but Windows programs usually don't have a special menu called Print. Printing is almost always handled with commands in the File menu.

By the way, you can learn lots more about dealing with files in *Excel For Dummies*. You might want to start with Chapter 1 and then check out the index for even more stuff.

File⇨Add Routing Slip...

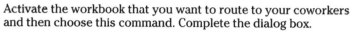

lets you prepare a worksheet to be circulated to others if you're working on a network. This command appears only if you are on a network.

How you use it

Activate the workbook that you want to route to your coworkers and then choose this command. Complete the dialog box.

File⇨Exit Routing Slip, File⇨Send

File⇨Close

Closes a worksheet. If you haven't saved it, Excel politely asks if you want to do so before it is removed from memory. If you no longer need a file, you can free up some memory by closing it.

If you hold down the Shift key when you choose this command, it miraculously turns into Close All. This option is a fast way to close down all the worksheets in memory in one fell swoop (you still get a warning if a worksheet has not been saved).

How you use it

Choose File⇨Close, and the active workbook is shut down. It's that easy.

File⇨Close All

File⇨Close All

Closes all open workbooks. **Note:** For this command to appear, you must hold down Shift when you choose the File menu.

File⇨Close

File⇨Edit Routing Slip...

 Lets you modify the routing slip attached to the workbook.
Note: This command appears only if the workbook has a routing slip attached.

How you use it

Activate the workbook that you want to route to your coworkers, choose this command, and modify the routing slip information.

File⇨Add Routing Slip, File⇨Send

File⇨Exit

Closes down Excel. If you have any unsaved work, Excel lets you know about it and gives you an opportunity to save it. Using this command is the proper way to exit Excel when you don't need to use it any more.

How you use it

Choose File⇨Exit and respond to any dialog boxes that Excel may present.

 Don't get in the habit of simply turning off your computer when your work is done. It's a good practice to exit all your applications first and then exit Windows. Wait until the computer's disk drive settles down and then turn off everthing on your system.

More stuff

Alt+F4 is a shortcut for this command, and it also works in most other Windows programs.

File⇨Find File...

Helps you locate a particular file and also copy and delete files.

How you use it

Choose File⇨Find, and Excel gives you a dialog box. Tell Excel what to search for (for example, *.xl?) and where to search (for example, drive C:) and then click on OK. Excel displays all the matching files. You can scroll through this list until you find the one you're looking for.

More stuff

Make sure you check the Include Subdirectories check box if you want to search the entire disk. When the file list is displayed, use the pull-down list labeled View to change what you see. Excel 5 files have a preview that lets you see the upper left part of the file. Click on the button labeled Commands to copy or delete files.

File⇨Macro...

Lets you select a macro to execute or edit. This command shows up only if no workbooks are active. It's the same as the Tools⇨Macro command.

Tools⇨Macro

File⇨New...

Creates a new Excel workbook. Using this command is generally how you start a new project.

How you use it

Choose File⇨New, and you get a blank workbook. (The shortcut key is Ctrl-N.)

More stuff

If you have one or more workbook templates defined (stored in your \XLSTART directory), Excel stops to ask you what type of workbook to create. Contrary to its name, this command does not actually create a file on disk. Rather, it creates a *potential* file in memory. You must use the File⇨Save command to actually save it as a file.

 Workbooks, by default, have 16 worksheets in them. If you want to change the number that appear in new workbooks, choose Tools⇨Options (General tab) and specify the number of sheets in a new workbook.

 File⇨Open, File⇨Save

File⇨Open...

 Loads a file from disk into Excel so that you can work on it. Using this command is how you work on something that's been saved to disk.

How you use it

Choose File⇨Open and then select the file you want to load. (The shortcut key is Ctrl-O.) The Open dialog box has a drop-down list box that lets you change the type of files that are displayed in the file list box. Normally, it displays only files with an XL* extension. You can change this extension if, for example, you want to load in a Lotus 1-2-3 file.

 You can select more than one file in the Open dialog box. The trick is to hold down the Ctrl key while you click on filenames. When all the files you want to open are highlighted, choose OK.

More stuff

Excel can read all files on your disk — but it can't always make sense of them. If your screen is filled with garbage after you load a file, it's a good sign that you loaded a file that Excel can't understand. A screenful of garbage is also symptomatic of trying to read an Excel file produced by a later version of Excel — for example, reading an Excel 5 file while using Excel 4.

If you check the Read Only box in the Open dialog box, you cannot save the file with the same name (use the File⇨Save As command to give it a different name). Using this command is a good way to make sure you don't accidentally mess up a perfectly good workbook.

If you tend to use the same worksheets all the time, you can save a few milliseconds of time each day by having Excel open them automatically. Simply move the worksheets to your \EXCEL\XLSTART directory, and Excel loads them automatically every time it starts up.

Excel can also open files created by other programs. Use the list box labeled List Files of Type to choose a different file type to display.

When you click on the File menu, Excel displays the names of the last four files you've worked on at the bottom of the menus. If you need to open one of these files, selecting it from the menu is much faster than opening it using normal methods. Oddly enough, I've discovered that many people have never noticed this.

File⇨New

File⇨*Page Setup...*

Lets you specify some options that determine how your printed output looks: change the orientation of the paper (landscape or portrait), change the paper size, change your margins, center the output on the page, print the spreadsheet row and column borders, remove the cell grids from printed output, ignore colors, specify a starting page number, scale the output, and change or remove headers and footers.

How you use it

Choose File⇨Page Setup, and select the desired options in the Page Setup dialog box. Don't overlook all those buttons along the right side — they lead to even more options. For example, the

Options button lets you choose the printer to use, which is relevant only if you have more than one printer installed. When you change settings with this command, they are in effect only for the current document and are saved along with the document.

If you find that your printouts are taking forever to come off the printer, try setting the Draft Quality option (in the Sheet tab). This option reduces the quality of the output, but it may be good enough for draft printouts.

File⇨Print, File⇨Print Preview

Look to *Excel For Dummies*, 2nd Edition for more explanation in Chapter 6,

---

File⇨Print Preview

Shows you, in the privacy of your own screen, exactly how your worksheet will look when it's printed. This preview includes headers and footers. Previewing can save you lots of time, since viewing your output on-screen is much faster than printing your work and *then* discovering that it was set up incorrectly. It also saves paper.

How you use it

Pretend as if you're going to print your work but choose File⇨Print Preview instead of File⇨Print. Excel displays the output in a full-screen window. The buttons at the top of the Preview window let you move to the next or previous page, zoom in or out, send it to the printer, go to the Setup dialog box, or quit the previewer.

More stuff

Notice that the mouse pointer is a magnifying glass in the preview window. You can click on a specific part of the previewed output to get a closer view. And you can use the scroll bars to move around in a magnified view.

File⇨Print

File ⇨ Print Report...

Lets you choose a predefined report for printing. This command is handy if you tend to make separate printouts of various views of your worksheet that you've defined. It eliminates the need to do all the setup work. Rather, you can do all the setup once and give it a name. Then, the next time you want to print the same thing, just choose the name of the report, and you're off to the races. This command works in conjunction with the View⇨View Manager command and the Tools⇨Scenarios command. Beginning users might find all this rather confusing.

How you use it

The key to using this command is to first use the View⇨View Manager command to create a view that includes the print area and any other print options that you want. A report can consist of a named view plus a named scenario (defined with the Tools⇨Scenarios command).

More stuff

This add-in is installed automatically when you install Excel and is loaded when you choose the File⇨Print Report command. If this command is not available, choose Tools⇨Add-Ins and select Report Manager.

File⇨Print, View⇨View Manager

File ⇨ Print...

Sends the current workbook, selected worksheets, or a range you specify to the printer. Using this command is the only way to get your worksheet onto paper (short of photographing the screen).

How you use it

Choose File⇨Print, and Excel displays a dialog box that lets you make your choices. When you close the dialog box, Excel sends the output to the printer.

TIP If you want to print out the formulas in your worksheet, choose Tools⇨Options (View tab) and click on the Formulas check box. Excel displays the actual formulas rather than their results. Print the worksheet as usual and then go back and use the Tools⇨Options command again and uncheck the Formula check box to get things back to normal.

More stuff

There are quite a few options in the Print dialog box. Fortunately, they are all pretty much self-explanatory. If not, click on the Help button for an explanation.

 TIP If you find that your printouts are taking forever to come off the printer, try setting the Draft Quality option (in the Sheet tab). This option reduces the quality of the output, but it may be good enough for draft printouts.

 REFERENCE File⇨Print Preview, File⇨Page Setup

 CROSS REFERENCE See Chapter 6 in _Excel For Dummies_, 2nd Edition for more on printing.

File⇨Record New Macro...

 TOOLBAR This command shows up only if no workbooks are active. It's the same as the Tools⇨Record Macro⇨Record New Macro command.

 REFERENCE Tools⇨Record Macro⇨Record New Macro

File⇨Save

 TOOLBAR Saves the current worksheet to disk. If what you're doing has any lasting value, using this command is how you can save it for posterity (or at least until you need to work on it again).

How you use it

Choose File⇨Save. If your document doesn't yet have an official name, Excel makes you give it one before saving it.

More stuff

The default name for a workbook document is BOOK*n*.XLS, where *n* is a number that starts with 1 and is incremented for every unnamed workbook you open. You can't save a file with this default name — and you probably wouldn't want to. The point of naming files is to make them somewhat meaningful to you and to describe what they do.

Ctrl+S is a shortcut for this command.

You should save your file at a time interval that corresponds to the maximum amount of time you're willing to lose. For example, if you don't mind losing up to an hour's work, save your file every hour. Most people choose to save their work more frequently than this.

If you can't remember to save (or you get really swept away by your work), use Excel's _Auto_ _Save_ command.

Tools⇨AutoSave, File⇨Save As

File⇨_Save_ _As_...

Saves the current worksheet to disk under a different name. Using this command is handy if you want to keep multiple versions of your work. You can save each successive version under a different name. That way, if you discover that you messed something up, you can always go back to an earlier version to recover from your stupidity.

How you use it

Choose File⇨Save As and enter a new name in the File Name box. You don't need to give an extension, since Excel supplies it for you.

More stuff

You can also use this command to make a backup copy of a file, simply by saving the file to a floppy disk (with the same name). After you do so, don't forget to save it again on your hard drive.

File⇨Save

File⇨Save Workspace...

Saves all open workbooks, including their window size and positions, to a disk file with the extension XLW. If you have a project that uses several workbooks, this command lets you quickly pick up where you left off.

How you use it

Choose File⇨Save Workspace and give a name for your workspace.

More stuff

 You can also use the File⇨Open command to open a workspace file.

File⇨Save, File⇨Open

File⇨Send...

 Sends or routes an Excel workbook file to someone else (or a group of people) on your network. This command appears only if you're on a network.

How you use it

Choose File⇨Send and specify your options in the dialog box.

More stuff

You can mail a workbook when you want to send it to one or more recipients simultaneously. If you want to send a workbook to a bunch of people sequentially or to automatically receive the workbook back, route the workbook instead.

 File⇨Add Routing Slip

File⇨_Summary Info..._

Lets you view or change the summary information for a workbook.

How you use it

Choose the command and make your changes. What you enter here is the stuff that shows up when you use the _File_⇨_Find_ File command.

More stuff

If you find that Excel isn't using your correct name, choose _Tools_⇨_Options_ (General tab) and enter your correct name.

File⇨_Find_ File

File⇨_Unhide..._

Lists hidden files and unhides the file you choose. This command is available only when there are no documents open; otherwise, you use the _Window_⇨_Unhide_ command.

Window⇨_Unhide_

Format Menu Commands

The commands under the F_o_rmat menu pretty much all deal with changing the looks of things.

As you might expect, _Excel For Dummies_ addresses worksheet formatting. In fact, Chapter 3 is devoted entirely to this issue.

Format⇨3-D View...

Lets you change the orientation and perspective of the chart. Sometimes columns in the back of a 3-D chart can be hidden by columns in the front. This command lets you manipulate the view so that you can see everything.

How you use it

When you have a 3-D chart displayed, choose Format⇨3-D View. Excel presents a rather imposing looking dialog box that lets you manipulate the viewing angle and perspective by clicking on arrows or entering values directly. As you do so, a 3-D chart replica (not your actual chart) moves according to your commands. Click on the Apply button to make the changes to your actual chart (you may have to move the dialog box out of the way to see it). When you're happy with the new look, choose OK.

It's fairly easy to completely mess up a 3-D chart with this command. If that happens to you, click on the Default button to get back to the original view.

More stuff

You might find it easier (or at least more fun) to simply click on one of the corners of a wall of a 3-D chart and simply drag it around. If you hold down the Ctrl key while you do this, you can also see the bars (not just the wall) move.

Format⇨AutoFormat...
(Chart version)

Applies one of several predefined AutoFormats to a chart. An AutoFormat goes much further than changing the chart type — it also changes colors, gridlines, and so on. You can even create your own AutoFormats so that a series of charts can all have the same look.

How you use it

When editing a chart, choosing this command pops up a dialog box with a list of Galleries. Choose a gallery, and Excel gives you miniature charts to choose from. Select the one you like and click on OK. The chart is reformatted and takes on the new look.

Format⇨Chart Type

Format⇨*AutoFormat...* (Worksheet version)

Applies one of 16 predefined table formats to a range of cells. Using this command is a very fast way to turn a dull table of words and numbers into an exciting, well-formatted table.

How you use it

Enter a table as you normally would, using values, formulas, and strings. Move the cell pointer anyplace in the table and choose Format⇨AutoFormat. Excel figures out the boundaries of the table and displays the AutoFormat dialog box with more than a dozen canned formats to choose from. Scroll through the list to get an idea of the end result.

More stuff

By default, this command changes the column widths — which may mess up stuff you have above or below the table. If you don't want all the formatting elements to be applied, click on the Options button and turn off any of the options. For example, if you don't want Excel to mess with the column widths, uncheck the Width/Height option.

Format⇨Cells

Format⇨_Cells..._

Lets you change just about everything that deals with the looks of a cell or range. **Note:** This command appears only if a cell or range is selected.

How you use it

Start by selecting the range you want to format. Choosing Format⇨Cells brings up a dialog box with six different tabs. (The shortcut key for this command is Ctrl-1.)Click on the tab you want and adjust the formatting. You can keep going back and forth among the tabs as long as you like. When you click on OK, the changes get made. The tabs are

Number	Changes the way the numbers appear (but doesn't change the actual value stored)
Alignment	Changes how information is aligned in cells
Font	Changes the font, size, and color
Border	Lets you put borders around cells or ranges
Patterns	Changes the shading used in the cells
Protection	Lets you make a cell hidden or locked so it can't be changed

More stuff

There are lots of options here. Fortunately, it's all pretty self-explanatory. If you can't figure out how to perform a particular formatting task, just click on the Help button for all the gory details. You can use toolbar icons for most of your formatting chores.

Format⇨_Chart Type..._

Changes the type of chart displayed.

How you use it

When you are editing a chart, choosing this command gives you a dialog box chock-full of different chart types. Choose the one you want, and the chart is transformed. Don't overlook the Options button, which gives you even more types to choose from.

More stuff

If you don't choose the Entire Chart option, only the selected data series is changed.

Format⇨AutoFormat

Format⇨Column⇨AutoFit Selection

Makes a column or columns wide enough to accommodate the widest entry.

How you use it

Select the cell or range that you're interested in and then choose Format⇨Column⇨AutoFit Selection. Excel changes the columns for the selected cells to match the widest entry in your selection.

More stuff

This command doesn't work if you select entire columns — you must select a range.

Double-clicking on the border makes the column wide enough to display the widest entry in the column.

Format⇨Column⇨Width, Format⇨Column⇨Standard Width

Format⇨Column⇨Hide

Hides a column or columns. Use this command if you have something in a column that you don't want to see. Or, you can hide columns that you don't want to be printed.

How you use it

Select at least one cell from the column or columns you want to hide and choose Format⇨Column⇨Hide.

More stuff

When columns are hidden, you can still refer to cells in them in your formulas.

Format⇨Column⇨Unhide

Format⇨Column⇨Standard Width...

Makes the width of a column or columns the standard width.

How you use it

Select at least one cell from the column or columns you want to change and choose Format⇨Column⇨Standard Width. A dialog box displays the standard width (in characters). Just click on OK to accept this width.

Format⇨Column⇨Width, Format⇨Column⇨AutoFit Selection

Format⇨Column⇨Unhide

Unhides a hidden column or columns.

How you use it

To unhide hidden columns, you must select cells to the left and to the right of the hidden columns. Then, choose the command, and the hidden columns reappear.

Format⇨Column⇨Hide

Format ⇨ Column ⇨ Width...

Changes the width of a column or columns. Some numbers are too wide to display in a cell, so you have to make the column wider to accommodate them. The width of a column does not affect how much information it can hold. It affects only how much of the cell contents show up on-screen.

How you use it

Select a cell or horizontal range of cells in the column or columns you want to adjust (you can also select entire columns). Choose the Format⇨Column⇨Width command and enter a value. The number you enter roughly corresponds to the number of default size characters that fit in a cell.

More stuff

You might find that changing column widths is easier if you drag the right border into the worksheet border (that has the column letters). If more than one column is selected, all the column widths are changed.

Format⇨Column⇨AutoFit Selection, Format⇨Column⇨Standard Width

Format ⇨ Object...

Changes the way a graphic object appears. **Note:** This command appears only if a graphic object is selected.

How you use it

Start by selecting the object you want to format. Choosing Format⇨Object brings up a dialog box with three different tabs. Click on the tab you want and adjust the formatting. You can keep going back and forth among the tabs as long as you like. When you click on OK, the changes get made. The tabs are

Patterns	Changes the borders and fill pattern used
Protection	Lets you lock an object so it can't be changed
Properties	Lets you specify how an object is sized or moved relative to the underlying cells; also lets you specify that the object won't print.

More stuff

You can select more than one object by holding down Ctrl as you click on objects. Using this command lets you format a bunch of objects with a single command. You can also get to this dialog box by simply double-clicking on the object.

Format⇨Placement⇨Bring to Front

Sends the selected object to the "top of the stack" when you are working with a group of graphic objects. It fully exposes an object that's partially hidden by other objects. **Note:** This command is available only when you have one or more objects selected.

How you use it

Select the object and then choose Format⇨Placement⇨Bring to Front.

Format⇨Placement⇨Send to Back

Format⇨Placement⇨Group

Combines several objects into one when you are working with objects drawn on a worksheet. If you're creating something that's made up of several different drawn objects, combining the objects into one object makes manipulating the drawing (changing the size or moving it) easier. **Note:** This command is available only when you have two or more objects selected.

How you use it

Select all the objects you want to include in the group; then choose Format⇨Placement⇨Group. To select multiple objects, hold down the Shift key while you select them or use the Drawing Selection tool on the Drawing toolbar to drag a rectangle around the objects you want to select.

Format⇨Placement⇨Ungroup

Format⇨Placement⇨Send to Back

Sends the selected object to the "bottom of the stack" when you are working with a group of graphic objects. The object may be obscured if other objects in the stack are larger than it is. **Note:** This command is available only when you have one or more objects selected.

How you use it

Select the object and then choose Format⇨Placement⇨Send to Back.

Format⇨Placement⇨Bring to Front

Format⇨Placement⇨Ungroup

When working with an object drawn on a worksheet that was grouped, this command ungroups the object into its original parts. **Note:** This command is available only when a grouped object is selected.

How you use it

Select the grouped object and issue the command Format⇨ Placement⇨Ungroup. The object is separated into its pieces.

Format⇨Placement⇨Group

Format⇨Row⇨AutoFit

Makes the row high enough to accommodate the tallest cell entry in the row. This command is useful if you made a row height larger and want to restore it to its normal size (which depends on the font used).

How you use it

Select at least one cell from the row or rows you want to adjust and choose the command.

More stuff

Double-clicking on the bottom border of the row's number does the same thing.

Format⇨Row⇨Height

Format⇨Row⇨Height...

Changes the height of a row or rows. Making a row higher than normal is a good way to add vertical spacing between rows — sometimes it is better than using blank rows.

How you use it

Select at least one cell from the row or rows you want to adjust and choose the command. Enter a row height in points (72 points is equivalent to one inch).

More stuff

You may find that clicking and dragging the bottom border of the row's number is easier.

Format⇨Row⇨AutoFit

Format⇨Row⇨Hide

Hides a row or rows. This command is useful if you have something in a row that you don't want to see. Or, you can hide rows that you don't want to be printed.

How you use it

Select at least one cell from the row or rows you want to hide and choose Format⇨Row⇨Hide.

More stuff

When rows are hidden, you can still refer to cells in them in your formulas.

Format⇨Row⇨Unhide

Format⇨Row⇨Unhide

Unhides a hidden row or rows.

How you use it

To unhide hidden rows, you must select cells above and below
the hidden rows. Then, choose Format⇨Row⇨Unhide, and the
hidden rows become unhidden rows.

Format⇨Row⇨Hide

Format⇨Selected [Object]...

Displays a formatting dialog box appropriate to the object
selected in a chart.

How you use it

Select a chart object and then choose this command (the wording
will vary, depending on what's selected). A dialog box that's
appropriate for the object appears.

More stuff

Double-clicking on an object gives you the same dialog box.

Format⇨Sheet⇨Hide

Hides a sheet or sheets. This command is useful if you don't want
a particular sheet cluttering up your workbook. All the information in a hidden sheet still works — you just can't see it.

How you use it

Activate the sheet you want to hide and then issue the command
Format⇨Sheet⇨Hide. The sheet disappears.

More stuff

You can't hide all sheets in a workbook; at least one must be
visible.

Format⇨Sheet⇨Unhide

Format⇨Sheet⇨Rename...

Changes the name of the current sheet. The sheet's name is what shows up on the tab at the bottom of the screen.

How you use it

Activate the sheet that you want to rename and then choose this command. Enter the new name, and it appears on the tab.

More stuff

You might find that double-clicking on the sheet tab and then entering the name is easier.

Format⇨Sheet⇨Unhide

Unhides a hidden sheet.

How you use it

Choose Format⇨Sheet⇨Unhide, and Excel displays a dialog box with a list of all hidden sheets. Pick the one you want to unhide and click on OK.

Format⇨Sheet⇨Hide

Format⇨Style...

Applies a predefined style to a cell or range of cells. It also lets you define and edit styles. Defining styles is a fast and easy way to apply consistent formats to cells and ranges.

How you use it

To create a style by example, format a cell as you want it and then choose Format⇨Style. Enter a name for the style in the dialog box and click on OK. After you do this, you can apply all those formats to another cell or range by issuing the Format⇨Style command and then specifying your style name.

More stuff

If you click on the Modify button, you get a new dialog box that lets you change specific parts of the style or create a style from scratch.

A fast way to change the default font for everything on a worksheet is to change the definition for Normal style. Choose Format⇨Style, click on the Modify button, and then click on the Font tab. Change the font to what you want and choose OK. Everything on the worksheet that hasn't been assigned to a different style changes to the new font.

Help Menu Commands

The Help menu commands access a specific part of Excel's on-line help system. Excel's help is very thorough, so do yourself a favor and don't overlook this resource.

The Help icon on the standard toolbar (it has an arrow and a question mark) is also useful. Click on the icon and then choose a command. Excel displays help about the command you chose.

If you need help to learn how to use help, you really need help. If so, read Chapter 1 in *Excel For Dummies*, 2nd Edition.

Help⇨About Microsoft Excel...

Displays a message that tells which version of Excel you're using, who the software is licensed to, the amount of memory, and whether your machine has a math coprocessor chip installed. If someone asks you what version of Excel you're using or if you have a math coprocessor installed, using this command will tell you in a flash.

More stuff

If you click on the System Info button, you can find out lots of
technical details about the current state of your computer. Most
of this information is completely meaningless to mere mortals.

Help ⇨ Contents

Displays the table of contents to Excel's on-line help system. If
you're looking for general help, the contents is a good place to
start.

How you use it

After choosing Help ⇨ Contents, just click on a topic that looks as
though it may be helpful. And don't overlook the buttons in the
Help window. You can use these buttons to go backward and
forward among the help topics and also jump to the window that
lets you search for a topic.

Help ⇨ Search for Help on

Help ⇨ Examples and Demos

Gives you access to nearly 100 examples and demonstrations on
various topics.

How you use it

After choosing Help ⇨ Examples and Demos, Excel displays a list
of topics. Click on a topic and choose a subtopic. Then, follow the
instructions on the screen. If all goes well, you should be moderately proficient in that topic when you're finished.

Help➪_Index_

Displays a book-like index that helps you locate a particular
help topic.

How you use it

After you choose _Help_➪_Index_, Excel displays a window that has
an index that looks remarkably like one you would find in the
back of a book. Click on an alphabetical button to jump quickly to
a particular letter. When you locate the topic of interest, click on
it. Excel treats you to more information than you probably want.

More stuff

You can get to this index window from any other Excel help
window by clicking on the Index button (just below the menu bar).

Help➪_Search for Help on_

Help➪_Lotus 1-2-3..._

Provides special help for people who have used Lotus 1-2-3. If you
know how to do something in 1-2-3 but can't figure out how to do
it in Excel, using this command will set you straight.

How you use it

Choose _Help_➪_Lotus 1-2-3_ and then choose the 1-2-3 command
that you know does what you want. Excel tells you how to do the
same thing using Excel's menus — and even does it for you in
some cases.

Help➪_Mutliplan..._

Provides special help for people who have used Microsoft's old
Multiplan spreadsheet (there must be one or two of them
remaining).

How you use it

Choose Help⇨Multiplan and then enter the specific Multiplan command. Excel tells you the equivalent.

Help⇨Quick Preview

Starts up an interactive session that introduces new users to Excel. This overview actually sums up what's available in Excel pretty well. It comes up automatically the first time you run Excel after you install it.

How you use it

After selecting Help⇨Quick Preview, just follow the directions on the screen.

Help⇨Search for Help on...

Lets you search the on-line help for a specific topic. Using this command is often the fastest way to get help on a specific topic or command. And, it may even be faster than using this book!

How you use it

After you choose the command, Excel runs the Help system and displays a dialog box. You can start typing a word or phrase, and Excel displays the matching topic in the box below. Or, you can just scroll through the topic list until you find the topic you want. Double-click on the topic to see a list of subtopics. Double-click on a subtopic to see information about it.

Help⇨Index

Help⇨_Technical Support_

Tells about the types of support Microsoft offers and how to get help when there's nowhere else to turn. If you're really stuck, the on-line help hasn't helped, the manual doesn't offer any solution, you can't find the office computer jock, and even _Excel For Dummies_ doesn't come through, using this command tells you how to contact Microsoft directly. There are several ways to do this. If you choose the telephone route, be prepared to spend some time on hold since lots of other people are in the same boat as you.

Insert Menu Commands

The Insert menu is where you go when you need to add (or remove) things from a worksheet or chart.

Insert⇨_Axes..._

Adds or remove axes from a chart.

How you use it

When you are editing a chart, choosing Insert⇨Axes brings up a dialog box with all the possible chart axes listed. To remove an axis, remove the check mark from the appropriate choice.

More stuff

You can change the appearance of a chart's axis by double-clicking on an axis.

Insert⇨_Cells..._

Lets you insert a new cell or range of cells.

How you use it

Select the cell or range where you want the new cells to be and then issue the command Insert⇨Cells. Excel responds with a dialog box that asks you how you want to shift the existing cells to make room for the new arrivals. You also have the opportunity to insert complete rows or columns.

Be careful when inserting a cell or range, since shifting cells around can cause problems elsewhere in the worksheet.

Insert⇨Columns, Insert⇨Rows

 Insert⇨Chart⇨As New Sheet

Creates a chart and inserts a new chart sheet to hold it.

How you use it

Select the range that you want to chart and then choose Insert⇨Chart⇨As New Sheet. Excel's ChartWizard kicks in to let you specify your options. Then, it inserts a new chart sheet right before the current sheet.

Insert⇨Chart⇨On This Sheet

Insert⇨Chart⇨On This Sheet

Creates a chart that's embedded right on the worksheet.

How you use it

Select the range that you want to chart and then choose Insert⇨Chart⇨On This Sheet. The status line instructs you to `Drag in document to create a chart`. After you drag the mouse to specify the chart's location, the ChartWizard appears. Go through the steps. When you're finished, the chart should appear in the location you specified.

More stuff

Once a chart is inserted on a worksheet, you can move it and resize it as you wish. To make changes to an embedded chart, double-click on it.

Insert⇨Chart⇨As New Sheet

Insert⇨Columns

Inserts one or more new columns.

How you use it

Select a cell or range that includes the area where you want the new columns. Issue the command Insert⇨Columns, and Excel shifts everything to the right to make room for the new column or columns. You can also start by selecting entire columns.

Insert⇨Cells

Insert⇨Data Labels...

Adds labels to a chart so that you can see what the various data points are.

How you use it

When you are editing a chart, choosing this command gives you a dialog box with several options. Choose the type of data labels you want and click on OK. Your chart is transformed.

More stuff

If you find that some of the data labels aren't positioned very well, you can simply click on a label and drag it to a better position. Also, you can format the data labels any way you like — double-click on a label to get to the formatting dialog box.

Insert⇨Error Bars...

Adds or removes error bars from a data series in a chart. Error bars are often used to indicate "plus or minus" information for each data point.

How you use it

When editing a chart, you need to select a data series before this command is available. Choosing the command gives you a dialog box with lots of options. Choose how you want the error bars displayed and then choose the amount. If you use the Help button, it will explain these options thoroughly. Click on OK, and the error bars appear.

More stuff

To get rid of error bars, select the data series, choose Insert⇨Error Bars, and then click on the None icon.

Insert⇨Trendline

Insert⇨Function...

Starts the Function Wizard so that you can enter a worksheet function as part of a formula.

How you use it

Choose Insert⇨Function and respond to the two dialog boxes.

More stuff

The Function Wizard keeps track of the worksheet functions that you use most frequently and displays them in the list box on the right side of the first Function Wizard dialog box.

You can check out Part IV of this book for a listing of Excel's built-in functions. Or, you can read Chapters 12 and 13 in *Excel For Dummies* for some real-life examples of functions that you might actually use at some point in your career.

Insert⇨Gridlines...

Adds or removes gridlines from a chart.

How you use it

When you are editing a chart, choosing this command brings up a dialog box with all the possible gridlines listed. To remove a set of gridlines, remove the check mark from the appropriate choice.

More stuff

You can change the way a set of gridlines looks by double-clicking on a gridline.

Insert⇨Legend

Adds a legend to a chart.

How you use it

When you are editing a chart, choose this command to add a legend to the chart. If the chart already has a legend, nothing happens.

More stuff

You can move a legend anywhere you like, and double-clicking on it lets you change its formatting.

Insert⇨Macro⇨Dialog

Inserts a dialog sheet.

How you use it

When you choose this command, Excel inserts a new sheet directly before the active sheet. This new sheet is a special type that contains a dialog box that you can customize.

More stuff

Creating custom dialog boxes is not something that beginners should try.

Insert⇨Macro⇨Module

Inserts a Visual Basic module sheet.

How you use it

When you choose this command, Excel inserts a new sheet directly before the active sheet. This new sheet is a special type that holds Visual Basic macro instructions.

Insert⇨Macro⇨MS Excel 4.0 Macro

Inserts a macro sheet on which you can create macros that are compatible with the Excel 4 XLM macro system.

How you use it

When you choose this command, Excel inserts a new sheet directly before the active sheet. This new sheet is a special type that holds macro instructions.

More stuff

This macro language is included for compatibility with previous versions. If you want to learn macro programming in Excel, you should use Visual Basic (not the Excel 4 XLM language).

Insert⇨Name⇨Apply...

Replaces ordinary cell references with range names that have been defined. This can make your formulas easier to read. If you define a name for a cell or range, Excel does not automatically replace normal references in formulas with the names. This command forces Excel to substitute the names for the references.

How you use it

Select the range that you want to work on and choose Insert⇨Name⇨Apply. Excel presents a dialog box with several options. Usually, you can just accept the default options.

Insert⇨Name⇨Create, Insert⇨Name⇨Define

Insert⇨Name⇨Create...

Automatically makes names for cells or ranges, using labels stored next to the cells or ranges to be named. Using this command is a fast way to create several range names at once.

How you use it

Make sure that the range names you want to create are stored as labels adjacent to their respective ranges. Select the names and the cells in the ranges to be named. Choose the Insert⇨Name⇨ Create command and tell Excel where the labels are relative to the cells. Click on OK.

If any of the range names already exist, Excel will ask if you want to replace the old name. Be careful with this, since changing a definition for a range name could have drastic results on your formulas.

Insert⇨Name⇨Define

Insert⇨Name⇨Define...

Lets you define a name for a cell or range or change a name that's been assigned. It also lets you change a range name or delete the name.

How you use it

Start by selecting the cell or range that you want to name. Choose the Insert⇨Name⇨Define command and enter a valid name (it must start with a letter and have no spaces). Click on OK. To change an existing name or references, choose the command and then click on the name you want to modify. Either edit the name or edit the reference displayed in the Refers to box. Click on the Add button. If you change a name of an existing range, you should delete the old name by using the Delete button.

 Be careful when you delete range names, since this operation can't be undone.

 You can also create a range name by using the Name box on the Formula bar. Simply select the cell or range you want to name, activate the Name box, type the name, and press Enter.

 Insert⇨Name⇨Create

Insert⇨Name⇨Paste...

When creating or editing a formula, using this command makes inserting a reference to a named cell or range easier. If you use named ranges or cells, you can insert such a name into a formula quickly. This command can also insert into your worksheet a reference list of all named cells and ranges.

How you use it

When you're building a formula and need to insert a name, choose Insert⇨Name⇨Paste and select the name from the list. To get a list of all names, move to an empty area of your worksheet, choose Insert⇨Name⇨Paste, and then click on the Paste List button.

If you use the Paste List button, Excel inserts a two-column list that will overwrite anything that gets in its way.

More stuff

Using the Name box to insert a name into a formula may be easier than using this command.

Insert⇨New Data...

Adds new data to an existing chart.

How you use it

When you are editing a chart, choose Insert⇨New Data. A dialog box asks for the range of data to add to the chart. You can enter the range directly or click in the text box and highlight it in a worksheet. Click on OK to get another dialog box that asks how you want to paste the data. Make your choice and click on OK. The chart shows its new data series.

More stuff

Another way to add new data to a chart is to select the range in a worksheet and drag it into the chart.

Insert⇨Note

Lets you attach a note to a cell. You can use cell notes to remind yourself of what you were thinking when you created a formula or to provide instructions to others.

How you use it

Move the cell pointer to the cell that you want to attach a note to; then choose Insert⇨Note. Enter the note and choose OK. Excel reminds you that a cell has a note by displaying a small red dot in the upper right corner of the cell. To read a note, activate the cell that has the note and choose Insert⇨Note.

More stuff

If you have a sound card and microphone attached to your computer, you can also record a voice note. But be careful. Long voice notes can make the file size get very large.

If you want your notes always to be visible, use the Text Box tool on the Standard toolbar to create free-floating notes.

Insert⇨_Object..._

Inserts an OLE object from another application into a workbook document.

How you use it

After you choose Insert⇨Object, choose one of the two tabs in the dialog box: Create New or Create From File. The Create New tab displays all available object types. The Create From File tab lets you insert a file. For example, to insert a new Word for Windows document into an Excel workbook, choose the Create New tab and select Microsoft Word 6.0 Document from the list. When you activate this object, Excel's menus and toolbars change to those used in Word for Windows.

More stuff

The object is stored in the Excel workbook file.

Insert⇨Page Break

Inserts a manual page break. This command is useful if you want to force page breaks in your printouts in places where they normally wouldn't break.

How you use it

Move the cell pointer to the place where you want the page break to occur and choose Insert⇨Page Break. Excel inserts a horizontal and vertical page break. If you want to insert only a horizontal page break, place the cell pointer in column A before you issue this command.

Insert⇨Remove Page Break

Insert⇨Picture...

Inserts into a worksheet a graphic image stored in a file.

How you use it

Choose Insert⇨Picture, and Excel displays a dialog box that lets you choose a graphics file. Locate the directory and filename. If you check the Preview Picture check box, you can see a thumbnail image of the selected file before you load it. Click on OK, and Excel inserts the image on your worksheet. You can then move and resize it to your liking.

More stuff

Excel supports a wide variety of graphics file formats, and you can even create your own with a drawing program (or use the Windows Paintbrush program). You can also use the Clipboard to copy images from other applications and then paste them onto a worksheet.

Insert ⇨ Remove Page Break

Removes a manual page break that you inserted with the
Insert⇨Page Break command. This command is available only
when the cell pointer is next to a manual page break.

How you use it

Move the cell pointer just below and/or to the right of a manual
page break and choose Insert⇨Remove Page Break. Excel
removes the page break.

More stuff

To remove all manual page breaks from a worksheet, select the
entire worksheet before choosing this command.

Insert⇨Page Break

Insert ⇨ Rows

Inserts one or more new rows into a worksheet.

How you use it

Select a cell or range that includes the area where you want the
new rows. Issue the Insert⇨Rows command, and Excel shifts
everything down to make room for the new row or rows. You can
also start by selecting entire rows.

More stuff

This command doesn't actually add new rows — a worksheet
always consist of exactly 16,384 rows. If the last row of a
worksheet contains any cell entries, this command won't work.

Insert⇨Cells

Insert ⇨ _Titles..._

 Lets you add any of five types of titles to a chart.

How you use it

When you are editing a chart, choosing this command pops up a dialog box that lists the five areas of a chart that can have a title. Choose the options you want and click on OK. Excel inserts some dummy text into your chart. Then, select the text it added and edit it so that it's what you want.

More stuff

Once the titles are inserted into your chart, you can move them around and change their formatting. Double-clicking is the direct route to the formatting dialog box.

Insert ⇨ _Trendline..._

 Adds a trendline to a data series in a chart. A trendline often makes spotting trends in your data easier (hence the name).

How you use it

When editing a chart, you must select a data series before this command is available. Choosing _Insert_ ⇨ _Trendline_ pops up a dialog box with several options. I can't go into the details here, but the _Help_ button will provide you with lots of information about your trendline options.

More stuff

 To get rid of a trendline, just select it and press Delete.

Insert ⇨ Error _Bars_

Insert⇨Worksheet

Inserts a new worksheet into the active workbook. Using additional worksheets in a workbook is a good way to organize your work.

How you use it

Issue the Insert⇨Worksheet command, and Excel inserts a new worksheet directly before the active sheet.

Tools Menu Commands

If Tim (the Toolman) Taylor used Excel, he would probably spend most of his time working with this menu. It contains a variety of tools to make your Excel sessions more productive.

Tools⇨Add-Ins...

Lets you choose which add-ins to load. It also lets you unload add-ins.

How you use it

After you choose this command, Excel presents a dialog box with a list of all installed add-ins. To load an add-in, just check its box. To unload an add-in, uncheck its box. Add-ins that are checked are loaded automatically whenever you start Excel.

More stuff

If you don't need an add-in, don't load it. Doing so just eats up memory and increases the time it takes for Excel to start up. You can also load an add-in using the File⇨Open command. But if you do it this way, you have no way to unload it.

File⇨Open

Tools⇨Assign Macro...

Lets you assign a macro to an object drawn on a worksheet. Using this command lets you, or someone else, execute a macro by clicking on an object placed on the worksheet. This command is usually easier to use than the Tools⇨Macro command to run a macro.

How you use it

First, put the object on the worksheet. The object can be a button, a graph, any geometric shape, or basically anything you draw on a worksheet using the tools in the Drawing toolbar. Select the object by clicking on it; then choose Tools⇨Assign Macro. Excel shows you a list of all the available macros. Choose one and select OK. From that point on, clicking on the object will run the macro.

 Make sure that the macro is always available when the workbook is loaded. In other words, the macro should be in the same workbook or in the Personal Macro Workbook.

Tools⇨Auditing⇨Remove All Arrows

 Cleans up your screen by removing all arrows left behind by the Tools⇨Auditing commands.

How you use it

Just issue the Tools⇨Auditing⇨Remove All Arrows command, and all the blue and red auditing arrows vanish.

Tools⇨Auditing⇨Show Auditing Toolbar

Displays the Auditing toolbar.

How you use it

Choose Tools⇨Auditing⇨Show Auditing Toolbar, and the Auditing toolbar appears. Using this toolbar is much easier than repeatedly using the Tools⇨Auditing commands.

Tools⇨*Auditing*⇨*Trace Dependents*

Tells you which formula cells depend on a particular cell.

How you use it

Select a cell and choose this command. Excel adds blue arrows to your worksheet identifying all the cells that directly depend on the selected cell.

More stuff

If you issue the command repeatedly, it will show additional levels of dependencies.

Tools⇨*Auditing*⇨*Trace Error*

Identifies the source of an error displaying in a cell.

How you use it

Activate a cell that's displaying an error value (for example, #NUM!). Excel displays a red arrow that shows the first precedent formula that also contains an error. Blue arrows point to cells with values that are used in the error-ridden formula.

Tools⇨Auditing⇨Trace Precedents

Tells you which cells are used by a particular formula cell.

How you use it

Select a cell that has a formula in it and choose this command. Excel adds blue arrows to your worksheet identifying the cells that the formula uses.

More stuff

The first time you choose this command, it shows the first-level precedents. You can keep issuing the command to show additional levels of precedents.

Tools⇨AutoSave...

Saves your work automatically at regular intervals. Using this command is really a good idea.

How you use it

Choose Tools⇨AutoSave and specify your preferences in the dialog box. The time you choose determines the maximum amount of work you can potentially lose if your system crashes or you experience a power failure.

More stuff

If this command isn't available, choose Tools⇨Add-Ins and check the AutoSave add-in.

File⇨Save

Tools⇨Data Analysis...

Opens the door to a slew of advanced analytical procedures. This command runs any of several sophisticated procedures (most of them statistical in nature) that use the data in your worksheet. Your options include three types of analysis of variance (ANOVA), correlation, covariance, descriptive statistics, exponential smoothing, *F*-test, Fourier analysis, histograms, moving average, random number generation, rank and percentile, regression, sampling, three types of *t*-tests, and a *z*-test.

How you use it

After you choose Tools⇨Data Analysis, choose the procedure you want and follow the directions on the screen.

The results of most of these procedures are in the form of a new range of data. These data are not linked to your original data. If any of your input numbers change, you have to repeat the procedure to update the results.

More stuff

If this command isn't available, choose Tools⇨Add-Ins and check the Analysis Toolpak add-in. If this doesn't appear as an option, you need to run Excel's Setup program and install it.

Tools⇨Goal Seek...

Determines the value required in a cell that will make a specific formula return a value that you want. Using this command saves you the trouble of using trial and error to find a value that makes a formula return the answer you want. You might think of this command as sort of a what-if in reverse. For example, if you have a worksheet set up to calculate the monthly payment for a loan, you can use Tools⇨Goal Seek to find the loan amount that results in a monthly payment that you can afford.

How you use it

Select the cell that has the formula for which you want to find a specific result, and choose the Tools⇨Goal Seek command. A dialog box asks for the value that you want the formula to produce and the cell that you want to vary. Click on OK to set Excel thinking. Once it finds the answer, you can replace the old value with the new one by choosing OK. Or, click on Cancel to keep the old value.

Be careful, since more than one value of an input cell can produce the same result.

Tools⇨Macro...

Lets you select a macro to execute or edit.

How you use it

When you choose the Tools⇨Macro command, Excel displays a dialog box with a list of macros from all the open workbooks. Click on the macro you want and choose the Run button to execute it. To modify the macro, click on the Edit button. The Options button lets you change some other things about the macro — its description, shortcut key, and whether it appears on the Tools menu.

Make sure that the macro you execute is appropriate. Macros are usually written for a very specific purpose, and you can't just go around running macros willy-nilly.

More stuff

Other ways to run a macro include pressing the key combination assigned to it, running it from the Tools menu (if it was assigned as such), and clicking on an object (including a macro button) that has been assigned a macro.

Tools⇨Assign Macro

Excel For Dummies, 2nd Edition tells you just enough about macros to get by in Chapter 10.

Tools⇨Options...

Lets you set a wide variety of options regarding how Excel works.

How you use it

When you choose this command, Excel displays a dialog box with the following tabs:

View	Determines what elements of Excel are shown
Calculation	Determines how the worksheets are calculated
Edit	Presents options having to do with cell editing
Transition	Determines how Excel behaves in response to certain 1-2-3 actions
General	Presents miscellaneous settings for Excel
Custom Lists	Lets you create custom lists for sorting or Autofill
Chart	Presents options for charting
Color	Determines what colors are available in Excel
Module General	Presents settings for Visual Basic modules
Module Format	Presents fonts and colors for Visual Basic modules

More stuff

You can switch among the tabs, and the changes take effect when you click on OK.

See Chapter 10 of *Excel For Dummies*, 2nd Edition for more.

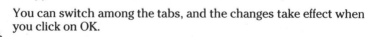

Tools⇨Protection⇨Protect Sheet...

Lets you protect various parts of the current worksheet so that they can't be changed. You can also assign a password that's required in order to unprotect these things. Using this command is one way to keep others (or yourself) from messing up a worksheet.

How you use it

Choose Tools⇨Protection⇨Protect Sheet and then select the options you want. Before you issue this command, use the Format⇨Cells (Protection tab) command to specify cells to protect or unprotect and Format⇨Object (Protection tab) to specify objects to protect or unprotect.

If you specify a password, don't forget it; otherwise, you'll never be able to make any changes to the worksheet.

Tools⇨Protection⇨Unprotect Sheet

Tools⇨Protection⇨Protect Workbook...

Prevents changes to the way a workbook is displayed and arranged — more specifically, the arrangement of the windows and the structure of the file. You can also assign a password that's required in order to unprotect these things.

How you use it

Choose Tools⇨Protection⇨Protect Workbook and then select the options you want (Structure and/or Windows). Enter a password if you desire.

More stuff

If you specify a password, don't forget it; otherwise, you'll never be able to make any changes to the worksheet.

Tools⇨Protection⇨Unprotect Workbook

Tools⇨_Protection_⇨_Unprotect Sheet..._

Makes a protected sheet an unprotected sheet. **Note:** This command appears only if the worksheet is protected.

How you use it

Just issue the command. If the sheet is protected with a password, you must enter the password.

Tools⇨Protection⇨Protect Sheet

Tools⇨_Protection_⇨_Unprotect Workbook..._

Makes a protected workbook an unprotected workbook. **Note:** This command appears only if the workbook is protected.

How you use it

Just issue the command. If the workbook is protected with a password, you must enter the password.

Tools⇨Protection⇨Protect Workbook

Tools⇨_Record Macro_⇨_Mark Position for Recording_

Lets you specify the location in an existing macro where a macro will be recorded to. This command is handy if you want to add on to an existing macro or insert new macro instructions in the middle of an existing macro.

How you use it

Activate the macro sheet (XLM Sheet or Visual Basic Module) and move the cell pointer to the location where you want recording to start. Then choose Tools⇨Record Macro⇨Mark Position for Recording. To start recording at that position, choose Tools⇨Record Macro⇨Record at Mark.

If you're using XLM macro, make sure that the cells below the position you mark are empty.

Tools⇨Record Macro⇨Record at Mark

Tools⇨Record Macro⇨Record at Mark

Starts macro recording at the location you specified with the Tools⇨Record Macro⇨Mark Position For Recording Command. This command doesn't create a new macro; rather, it lets you add on to or replace part of one that already exists. **Note:** This command is available only if you marked a position for recording.

How you use it

Choose this command and your actions are recorded.

Tools⇨Record Macro⇨Record New Macro

Tools⇨Record Macro⇨Record New Macro...

Starts recording a new macro. Using this command is how you record your actions to be played back later. In other words, you can create a macro with this command if you don't want to type in all the macro instructions manually.

How you use it

Choose Tools⇨Record Macro⇨Record New Macro. A dialog box lets you assign a name to the macro, specify a shortcut key combination, create a command for the Tools menu, and tell where you want to record it (either in the current workbook, your Personal Macro Workbook, or in a new workbook). This command also lets you choose which macro language to record in — Visual Basic, or the old XLM macro language. If you're new to macros, you're better off using Visual Basic.

More stuff

While you're recording the macro, Excel displays the word Recording in the status bar and also pops up a single-icon toolbar. Clicking on the tool in this toolbar stops macro recording.

Tools⇨Record Macro⇨Record at Mark

Tools⇨Record Macro⇨ Stop Recording

Stops the macro recording process. **Note:** This command appears only while you're recording a macro.

Tools⇨Record Macro⇨ Use...

Toggles the way macros are recorded — from absolute references to relative references. When you choose relative references, Excel records cell references relative to the current cell. It uses a different method to do this. Rather than record an absolute cell reference such as A4, it records cell references in terms of offsets from the starting cell. Usually, macros recorded in this way are more general than those recorded using the default absolute record method.

How you use it

Choosing the command puts a check mark next to the menu item — this means that the macro will be recorded using relative references. If there is no check mark next to the menu item, macros will be recorded using absolute references. You can choose this command either before you start recording or while you're recording.

Tools⇨Scenarios...

Makes it easy to keep track of various sets of input cells that you may want to change to calculate different scenarios. Spreadsheets are particularly adept at showing various outcomes (or scenarios) based on changing input values. This command lets you give meaningful names to sets of assumptions and then instantly change them. For example, your annual sales forecast might have *best_case, worst_case*, and *most_likely* scenarios. This command automates the process of plugging in a bunch of different values.

How you use it

Set up your spreadsheet with formulas and input values that affect the formulas. Select all the input values (changing cells) for a particular scenario and then choose Tools⇨Scenarios and click on Add. You need to provide a name for that particular scenario. Exit with OK. Then, you can insert different values for the changing cells and use the Tools⇨Scenarios command to create a name for this scenario. Or, you can change the values in the dialog box. To display the worksheet using a particular scenario, choose the Show button.

More stuff

You can also create a summary report that shows how one or more formula cells change under each of the scenarios.

Tools⇨Solver...

 Lets you find one or more solutions to a problem that's set up properly in your worksheet. Solver lets advanced users who know what they're doing solve a variety of linear and nonlinear analysis problems.

How you use it

Sorry, but this one is way beyond the scope of this book.

More stuff

 If this command doesn't appear, choose Tools⇨Add-Ins and select Solver. If Solver doesn't appear in the list of add-ins, you need to rerun Excel's Setup program and tell it to install the Solver.

Tools⇨Goal Seek

Tools⇨Spelling...

 Starts Excel's spelling checker on the active worksheet. Use this command to avoid the embarrassment and potential public humiliation of turning in work with misspelled words.

How you use it

Select the range to be checked. If you don't do so, Excel checks the entire worksheet. Whenever Excel finds a word that it doesn't recognize, it displays the word along with some guesses. You can double-click on a guess to replace the word or use the buttons for other options.

Just because your worksheet passes the spelling checker doesn't mean that everything is OK. Spelling checkers don't have any intelligence and cannot warn you of a heading such as *United Snakes Production* when you meant to say *Untied States Production*.

View Menu Commands

The commands on the <u>V</u>iew menu determine what sorts of things are visible on your screen.

<u>V</u>iew⇨<u>F</u>ormula Bar

Toggles the formula bar on and off. In most cases, the formula bar should always be visible.

How you use it

When a check mark appears to the left of this command, the formula bar is visible. If there is no check mark, the formula bar is hidden.

<u>V</u>iew⇨F<u>u</u>ll Screen

 Toggles full screen mode on and off. If you want to see the maximum amount of information, going to full screen mode does the trick.

How you use it

Choose <u>V</u>iew⇨F<u>u</u>ll Screen, and Excel hides everything except the workbook windows and the menu bar. It also displays a single-icon toolbar that lets you get out of full screen mode.

More stuff

 If your goal is to see more information on the screen, you should also consider changing the zoom factor.

<u>V</u>iew⇨<u>Z</u>oom

View⇨Sized with Window

Toggles whether a chart's size will vary with the size of the window. **Note:** This command is available only when a chart sheet is active.

How you use it

Normally, the size of a chart is independent of the window size. If you want the chart's size to change when you resize the window, choose this command. When the command has a check mark to the left of it, the chart will be sized with the window.

View⇨Status Bar

Toggles the status bar on and off. You can see an additional row or two if you hide the status bar.

How you use it

When a check mark appears to the left of this command, the status bar is visible. If there is no check mark, the status bar is hidden.

View⇨Toolbars...

Lets you choose which toolbars to display and also set some other toolbar options.

How you use it

When you choose View⇨Toolbars, Excel displays a list of all available toolbars. Put a check next to the toolbars that you want to display and remove the check mark from those that you don't want.

More stuff

This command also lets you toggle toolbar color on and off, change the size of the toolbar buttons, and turn off the Tool Tips (Tool Tips appear when you move the mouse pointer over a toolbar icon and leave it there for about a second).

Another way to hide or display specific toolbars is to right-click on any toolbar and choose from the shortcut menu.

 *View⇨View Manager...*

 Lets you save particular view settings as a named view. A view consists of the window size and position, frozen panes or titles, outlining, zoom percentage, the active cell, print area, and many of the settings in the Options dialog box (which you access with the Tools⇨Options command).

How you use it

Get your worksheet set up the way you want it, then choose View⇨View Manager. Click on Add and enter a name for your view. Change different settings and repeat these steps, giving a different name for each view. To display the worksheet with a particular view setting, choose View⇨View Manager, select the named view, and click on Show.

More stuff

 This command works hand-in-hand with the File⇨Print Report command.

File⇨Print Report

 View⇨Zoom...

 Lets you change the screen magnification. Using this command can give you a bird's-eye view of your worksheet, so that you can get an overview of how it's laid out and how objects and graphs are placed. Or, you can use this command to blow up your worksheet so that you can read the text from across the room.

This command does not affect the way a worksheet looks when it is printed. If you want to shrink or increase the size of your printed output, use the File⇨Page Setup command and adjust the Scaling parameter.

How you use it

Choose View⇨Zoom and then pick a zoom factor between 10 percent and 400 percent.

More stuff

You might also find the Fit Selection option useful. Select a range of cells, issue the View⇨Zoom command, and then choose Fit Selection. This automatically sets the zoom factor so that all the selected cells fit on the screen.

View⇨Full Screen

Window Menu Commands

The Window menu commands deal with the way Excel's windows appear and operate.

Window⇨Arrange...

Arranges the windows of all active documents neatly on-screen. Using this command is a quick way to see all the open documents. You can then drag and resize them as you like. **Note:** This command is not available if all windows are minimized or hidden.

How you use it

Choose Window⇨Arrange, and Excel displays a dialog box with four options: Tiled (arrange them like floor tiles), Horizontal (arrange them horizontally), Vertical (arrange them vertically), or Cascade (stack them up neatly with all the titles visible). Another option lets you just arrange the windows of the active document.

Window⇨Arrange Icons

Lines up all the Window icons neatly across the bottom of the screen. **Note:** This command is not available if no windows are minimized.

How you use it

Just choose Window⇨Arrange Icons, and Excel does its housekeeping.

Window⇨Freeze Panes

Freezes the row(s) above the active cell and the column(s) to the left of the active cell so that they are always visible no matter where you are. This command can be handy if you want to be able to see row and/or column headers no matter where you are in your worksheet. **Note:** This command is not available if the panes are already frozen.

How you use it

Move the cell pointer to the cell at which you want the freezing to occur. Choose Window⇨Freeze Panes, and the column(s) and row(s) to the left and top of the cell pointer are frozen in place.

 Chapter 5 of *Excel For Dummies*, 2nd Edition offers more on this subject.

Window⇨Hide

Hides the current document window. This command can get a window out of your way, yet keep it in memory ready to be used when necessary.

How you use it

Choose Window⇨Hide, and the active document is hidden.

Window⇨New Window

Creates a new "view" of the current document in a new window. This command is handy if you would like to view two or more parts of a worksheet at once.

How you use it

Choose Window⇨New Window, and Excel opens another window with the same worksheet.

Window⇨Remove Split

Unsplits a window that has been split with the Window⇨Split command. **Note:** This command does not appear if the window is not split.

How you use it

Just choose Window⇨Remove Split, and the splits are gone.

More stuff

Dragging the pane to the side of the screen to get rid of the split may be easier.

Window⇨Split

Splits the current document into four panes, at the active cell. Using this command is a way to view two or four parts of a worksheet at once. **Note:** This command does not appear if the window is already split.

How you use it

Move the cell pointer to the place where you want the split to occur and choose Window⇨Split.

More stuff

You may find that dragging the small black bar at the top of the vertical scroll bar or to the left of the horizontal scroll bar is an easier way to split the screen.

Window⇨_Unfreeze Panes_

Returns things back to normal after you chose the _Window_⇨_Freeze_ Panes command. **Note:** This command is not available if the panes are not frozen.

How you use it

Just choose _Window_⇨Unfreeze Panes, and Excel thaws your worksheet in a flash.

Window⇨_Unhide..._

Lets you choose a hidden window to unhide. You can use this command to reveal a window that has been hidden with the _Window_⇨_Hide_ command.

How you use it

Choose _Window_⇨_Unhide_, and Excel displays a list of all hidden windows. Choose the one you want to reveal and click on OK.

Part III:
Dummies Guide to Excel's Toolbars

A carpenter has a toolbox, a painter has a palette, and a spreadsheet junkie has a toolbar. Getting into the habit of using Excel's toolbars will save you lots of time and effort over the long haul. I found that many people ignore these icons because they don't know what the icons do and they're afraid that clicking the wrong one will screw something up. Actually, this fear is pretty much ungrounded, since you can use the Edit⇨Undo command to reverse the effects of almost any disaster caused by a toolbar icon.

Chapter 11 of *Excel For Dummies,* 2nd Edition tells you even more about these toolbars.

About Excel's Toolbars

Excel 5.0 ships with thirteen ready-to-use toolbars (although a few are pretty wimpy, with only one tool). You can also customize these toolbars by removing tools you don't need and adding other ones. And if you're really ambitious, you can create new toolbars which perform tasks that you do most often.

To display a toolbar, use the View⇨Toolbars command and select the toolbar you want. You can also click the right mouse button anywhere in a toolbar (except on an icon) to get a shortcut menu of toolbars. You can have more than one toolbar displayed, and you can move them wherever you like on-screen.

Customizing a toolbar is quite easy — and you will find lots of useful tools that aren't on any of the prebuilt toolbars. First, make sure the toolbar you want to modify is displayed. Then, choose the View⇨Toolbars command and click on the Customize button. A new dialog box pops up. The available tools are arranged by categories. Select a category and then simply drag a tool to the toolbar that you're customizing. To get rid of a tool, just drag it off the toolbar. When you get the toolbar the way you want it, choose Close.

 There's no excuse for shunning toolbars by saying you don't remember what a particular icon does. When you move the mouse over a toolbar icon and wait about one second, Excel pops up a little box with the tool's name. The status bar at the bottom of the screen also displays a one-line description of the tool.

Now it's time to belly up to the toolbar and see what Excel is serving.

Auditing Toolbar

If you're at the point where you need help analyzing your formulas, this toolbar will save lots of trips to the menu.

	**Trace Precedents**	Shows cells that a formula refers to by drawing arrows to the cells.
	Remove Precedent Arrows	Takes away one level of precedent arrows.

Trace Dependents Shows formulas that use a particular cell by drawing arrows to the cells.

Remove Dependent Arrows Takes away one level of dependent arrows.

Remove All Arrows Takes away all auditing arrows.

Trace Error Shows cells that are causing an error in a particular cell by drawing arrows to the troublesome cells.

Attach Note Lets you read or add a cell note.

Show Info Window Displays Excel's Info Window that gives you lots of details about the active cell.

Chart Toolbar

The Chart toolbar appears automatically whenever you activate a chart sheet or double-click on an embedded chart.

Chart Type Lets you change a chart's type. This tool expands to show 14 chart types, and it can be torn off and moved anywhere on-screen.

Default Chart Creates a chart using the default chart type.

ChartWizard Starts up the Chart Wizard so that you can create a chart.

Horizontal Gridlines Adds or removes horizontal gridlines from a chart.

Legend Adds or removes the legend from a chart.

Drawing Toolbar

The Drawing toolbar is useful if you want to add drawings or create objects on your worksheets or charts.

Line	Draws a straight line.
Rectangle	Draws a rectangle or a square.
Ellipse	Draws an oval or a circle.
Arc	Draws an arc or a circle segment.
Freeform	Draws freehand and polygon shapes.
Text Box	Draws a text box on a worksheet or lets you add unattached text to a chart.
Arrow	Creates an arrow on a worksheet or macro sheet or puts an arrow on the active chart.
Freehand	Draws freehand lines.
Filled Rectangle	Draws a rectangle or square that's filled with the window background pattern and color.
Filled Ellipse	Draws an oval or circle that's filled with the window background pattern and color.
Filled Arc	Draws a circle segment that's one-quarter of a full circle and filled with the window background pattern and color.
Filled Freeform	Draws a polygon that's filled with the window background pattern and color.
Create Button	Draws a button to which you can assign a macro. When you click on the button, the macro executes.

▣	**Drawing Selection**	Selects one or more graphic objects.
▣	**Bring To Front**	Places one or more selected objects in front of all other objects.
▣	**Send To Back**	Places one or more selected objects behind all other objects.
▣	**Group Objects**	Combines a group of graphic objects into a single object.
▣	**Ungroup Objects**	Separates grouped objects into individual objects.
▣	**Reshape**	Lets you to change the shape of a polygon.
▣	**Drop Shadow**	Adds a shadow to the bottom and the right side of a selected cell or range.
▣	**Pattern**	Lets you change the pattern shown in objects or cells.

Formatting Toolbar

The Formatting toolbar has lots of useful formatting tools on it. It's displayed by default, right under the standard toolbar.

Font Arial		Lets you change the font used in the selection.
10	**Font Size**	Lets you change the size of the font used in the selection.
B	**Bold**	Toggles the bold attribute of the characters in the selection.
I	**Italic**	Toggles the italic attribute of the characters in the selection.
U	**Underline**	Toggles the underline attribute of the characters in the selection.

Align Left

Makes the characters in the selection left-aligned.

Center

Makes the characters in the selection centered.

Align Right

Makes the characters in the selection right-aligned.

Center Across Columns

Centers the text in a cell across a horizontal range of cells.

Currency Style

Applies the Currency style to the selection.

Percent Style

Applies the Percent style to the selection.

Comma Style

Applies the Comma style to the selection.

Increase Decimal

Increases the number of decimal places shown in the selection.

Decrease Decimal

Decreases the number of decimal places shown in the selection.

Borders

Adds, changes, or takes away borders in the selection. This tool expands to show 12 border styles, and it can be "torn off" and moved anywhere on-screen.

Color

Sets or changes the background color in the selection. This tool expands to show 56 colors, and it can be "torn off" and moved anywhere on-screen.

Font Color

Sets or changes the color of the text in the selection. This tool expands to show 56 colors, and it can be "torn off" and moved anywhere on-screen.

Forms Toolbar

The Forms toolbar is intended primarily for advanced users who develop custom dialog boxes. Most of the tools add controls to a dialog box. However, you can use some of these tools directly on a worksheet. For example, you can insert a scroll bar control on your worksheet and set it up so that moving the scroll bar changes the value in a cell — and you don't even have to use a macro to perform this feat!

Aa	**Label**	Adds a control that contains fixed-font text.
abl	**Edit Box**	Adds an edit box control.
	Group Box	Adds a group box control to hold other objects.
	Create Button	Adds a button control.
x	**Check Box**	Adds a check box control.
●	**Option Button**	Adds an option button control.
	List Box	Adds a list box control.
	Drop-Down	Adds a drop-down list box control.
	Combination List-Edit	Adds a combination list box and edit box control.
	Combination Drop-Down Edit	Adds a combination drop-down list and edit box control.
	Scroll Bar	Adds a scroll bar control.
◆	**Spinner**	Adds a spinner control.
	Control Properties	Lets you adjust the properties of the selected control.
	Edit Code	Switches you to the Visual Basic macro that the control uses (or creates a macro if none exists).

Toggle Grid   Toggles the grid displayed in a dialog box (this also works with worksheet gridlines).

Run Dialog   Tests the dialog box.

Full Screen Toolbar

Talk about wimpy toolbars — the Full Screen toolbar has but a single icon.

Full Screen   Switches Excel from full-screen view to normal view (or vice versa). When you switch to full-screen view using the View⇨Full Screen command, this toolbar appears automatically — providing an easy way to get things back to normal.

Microsoft Toolbar

The Microsoft toolbar is more like an advertisement for Microsoft's products. It lets you launch (or switch to) any of several programs — all from Microsoft. Obviously, the appropriate program must be installed on your system for the tool to work.

Microsoft Word   Launches or switches to Word (a word processing program).

Microsoft PowerPoint   Launches or switches to PowerPoint (a presentation graphics program).

Microsoft Access   Launches or switches to Access (a database program).

Microsoft FoxPro   Launches or switches to FoxPro (a database program).

Microsoft Project   Launches or switches to Project (a project management program).

Microsoft Schedule+   Launches or switches to Schedule+ (an appointment scheduling program).

Microsoft Mail   Launches or switches to Mail (an electronic mail program).

Query and Pivot Toolbar

If you've discovered the wonderful world of pivot tables, you're probably already familiar with the Query and Pivot toolbar because it pops up automatically when you create a pivot table.

PivotTable Wizard   Starts up the Pivot Table Wizard.

PivotTable Field   Lets you adjust a field in a pivot table.

Ungroup   Ungroups grouped items in a pivot table.

Group   Groups items in a pivot table.

Hide Detail   Hides the detail of grouped items in a pivot table.

Show Detail   Shows the detail of grouped items in a pivot table.

Show Pages   Copies each page field item in a pivot table to a separate worksheet.

Refresh Data   Updates the pivot table with new data from a the database.

Standard Toolbar

The Standard toolbar is displayed by default.

New Workbook   Creates a new workbook.

Open

Displays the Open dialog box so that you can load a document from disk.

Save

Saves changes made to the active document.

Print

Prints the active document according to the options specified in the Print dialog box.

Print Preview

Shows what your printed output will look like.

Spelling

Starts the spelling checker.

Cut

Removes the selection and places it on the Clipboard.

Copy

Copies the selected cells, characters, or objects onto the Clipboard.

Paste

Pastes into the selection only the cell formats from the cells that you have copied onto the Clipboard.

Format Painter

Lets you easily copy formats and paste them to other cells.

Undo

Reverses the effect of the last command.

Repeat

Repeats the last command.

AutoSum

Inserts into the active cell a formula with the SUM function and a proposed sum range. The proposed range is based on the data above or to the left of the active cell.

Function Wizard

Starts the Function Wizard so that you can enter a worksheet function into a formula.

Sort Ascending

Sorts the active data table in ascending order, using the column that contains the active cell.

	Sort Descending	Sorts the active data table in descending order, using the column that contains the active cell.

ChartWizard — Starts the ChartWizard so that you can edit an embedded chart or chart sheet or create a new chart as an embedded object on a worksheet.

Text Box — Adds a free-floating box in which you can enter text.

Drawing — Displays or hides the Drawing toolbar.

Zoom Control — Lets you adjust the zoom factor of the current window.

`100%`

TipWizard — Displays or hides the TipWizard toolbar.

Help — Adds a question mark (?) to the mouse pointer. When you place the new pointer over a command name or screen region and click the mouse button, you get information about that command or screen region.

Stop Recording Toolbar

The Stop Recording toolbar has a grand total of one tool on it. The toolbar displays automatically when a macro is paused.

Stop Macro — Stops recording a macro.

TipWizard Toolbar

The TipWizard toolbar is where you get all those nifty little tips. You can toggle it on or off by clicking on the TipWizard icon on the Standard toolbar.

> 1) Click any toolbar with the right mouse button to display a shortcut menu for showing, hiding, and customizing toolbars.

TipWizard Box	Displays a list of tips that are relevant to the tasks you've been performing.
Tip Help	Displays more information about the tip currently being displayed.

Visual Basic Toolbar

The Visual Basic toolbar is for Visual Basic macro mavens.

Insert Module	Inserts a new Visual Basic module directly before the current sheet.
Menu Editor	Lets you edit the menus.
Object Browser	Displays the Object Browser dialog box so you can determine objects, properties, and methods.
Run Macro	Starts the current macro.
Step Macro	Steps through the current macro one line at a time.
Resume Macro	Resumes execution of a macro that has been paused.
Stop Macro	Stops execution of a macro or stops macro recording.
Record Macro	Starts the process of recording your actions into a macro.
Toggle Breakpoint	Makes the current line a breakpoint or removes its breakpoint status.
Instant Watch	Displays the value of an expression or variable while the macro is running.
Step Into	When stepping through a macro, executes the next statement.
Step Over	When stepping through a macro, skips over the next statement.

Workgroup Toolbar

The tools on the Workgroup toolbar might be useful if you run Excel on a network.

Find File Lets you locate a file (equivalent to the File⇨Find File command).

Routing Slip Adds or edits a routing slip attached to the active workbook.

Send Mail Sends the current workbook to one or more other users on your network.

Update File Updates a read-only workbook to the most recent version saved.

Toggle Read Only Toggles the read-only status of a workbook.

Scenarios Lets you choose a scenario to display or define a scenario.

Part IV:
Dummies Guide to Excel's Worksheet Functions

Excel provides a boatload of built-in worksheet functions — far too many for people who write books about Excel. You can use these functions to do special calculations and often simplify your formulas.

For more background on Excel's functions, check out Chapters 12 and 13 in *Excel For Dummies,* 2nd Edition.

Excel's Worksheet Functions

Most worksheet functions take arguments, which are always enclosed in parentheses and separated by commas (with no spaces in between). Even if a function doesn't need an argument, you must insert a pair of empty parentheses. The arguments can be references to cells or actual numbers or text strings. When Excel evaluates a function, it returns a single value or label.

Because Excel's on-line help is particularly good for functions, I don't go into the details here. Rather, I just list the functions, by category. To learn the exact details for a function, use the Function Wizard. For example, if you want to write a formula that returns the second largest value in a range, you can start by browsing through the functions in the Math & Trigonometry and Statistical sections of this chapter. You'll eventually find a function called LARGE, which returns the *k*th largest value in a range. To learn how to use this function do the following:

1. Select the Insert⇨Function command (or click on the Function Wizard tool) to bring up Excel's Function Wizard.

2. Choose the Statistical function category in the dialog box.

3. Scroll through the function list until you locate LARGE and click on it.

4. Click on the Next button to move on to Step 2 of the Function Wizard. It tells you that this function requires two arguments.

5. To learn more about the arguments, click on the Help button.

6. After you enter the arguments, click on OK. Excel inserts the function in the active cell.

The following pages summarize these worksheet functions. The functions are listed in alphabetical order within each category. The categories are

- Database
- Date & Time
- DDE & External
- Engineering
- Financial
- Information

- Logical
- Lookup & Reference
- Math & Trigonometry
- Statistical
- Text

Note: Some of these functions (particularly the more obscure ones) require that the Analysis ToolPak add-in be loaded. If the function returns #NAME?, Excel cannot find the function. To make the function available, use the Tools⇨Add-Ins command and select Analysis ToolPak from the displayed list. If you cannot find that add-in in the list, you need to run Excel's Setup program and tell it that you want to install it.

Database

DAVERAGE	DSTDEV
DCOUNT	DSTDEVP
DCOUNTA	DSUM
DGET	DVAR
DMAX	DVARP
DMIN	SQLREQUEST
DPRODUCT	SUBTOTAL

Date & Time

DATE	HOUR
DATEVALUE	MINUTE
DAY	MONTH
DAYS360	NETWORKDAYS
EDATE	NOW
EOMONTH	SECOND

Date & Time (continued)

TIME	WORKDAY
TIMEVALUE	YEAR
TODAY	YEARFRAC
WEEKDAY	

DDE & External

CALL
REGISTER.ID
SQLREQUEST

Engineering

BESSELI	HEX2BIN
BESSELJ	HEX2DEC
BESSELK	HEX2OCT
BESSELY	IMABS
BIN2DEC	IMAGINARY
BIN2HEX	IMARGUMENT
BIN2OCT	IMCONJUGATE
COMPLEX	IMCOS
CONVERT	IMDIV
DEC2BIN	IMEXP
DEC2HEX	IMLN
DEC2OCT	IMLOG10
DELTA	IMLOG2
ERF	IMPOWER
ERFC	IMPRODUCT
GESTEP	IMREAL

Engineering (continued)

IMSIN	OCT2BIN
IMSQRT	OCT2DEC
IMSUB	OCT2HEX
IMSUM	SQRTPI

Financial

ACCRINT	FVSCHEDULE
ACCRINTM	INTRATE
AMORDEGRC	IPMT
AMORLINC	IRR
COUPDAYBS	MDURATION
COUPDAYS	MIRR
COUPDAYSNC	NOMINAL
COUPNCD	NPER
COUPNUM	NPV
COUPPCD	ODDFPRICE
CUMIPMT	ODDFYIELD
CUMPRINC	ODDLPRICE
DB	ODDLYIELD
DDB	PMT
DISC	PPMT
DOLLARDE	PRICE
DOLLARFR	PRICEDISC
DURATION	PRICEMAT
EFFECT	PV
FV	RATE

Financial (continued)

RECEIVED	VDB
SLN	XIRR
SYD	XNPV
TBILLEQ	YIELD
TBILLPRICE	YIELDDISC
TBILLYIELD	YIELDMAT

Information

CELL	ISNA
COUNTBLANK	ISNONTEXT
ERROR.TYPE	ISNUMBER
INFO	ISODD
ISBLANK	ISREF
ISERR	ISTEXT
ISERROR	N
ISEVEN	NA
ISLOGICAL	TYPE

Logical

AND	NOT
FALSE	OR
IF	TRUE

Lookup & Reference

ADDRESS	LOOKUP
AREAS	MATCH
CHOOSE	OFFSET
COLUMN	ROW
COLUMNS	ROWS
HLOOKUP	TRANSPOSE
INDEX	VLOOKUP
INDIRECT	

Math & Trigonometry

ABS	FLOOR
ACOS	GCD
ACOSH	INT
ASIN	LCM
ASINH	LN
ATAN	LOG
ATAN2	LOG10
ATANH	MDETERM
CEILING	MINVERSE
COMBIN	MMULT
COS	MOD
COSH	MROUND
COUNTIF	MULTINOMIAL
DEGREES	ODD
EVEN	PI
EXP	POWER
FACT	PRODUCT
FACTDOUBLE	QUOTIENT

Math & Trigonometry (continued)

RADIANS	SUM
RAND	SUMIF
ROMAN	SUMPRODUCT
ROUND	SUMSQ
ROUNDDOWN	SUMX2MY2
ROUNDUP	SUMX2PY2
SERIESSUM	SUMXMY2
SIGN	TAN
SIN	TANH
SINH	TRUNC
SQRT	

Statistical

AVEDEV	FDIST
AVERAGE	FINV
BETADIST	FISHER
BETAINV	FISHERINV
BINOMDIST	FORECAST
CHIDIST	FREQUENCY
CHIINV	FTEST
CHITEST	GAMMADIST
CONFIDENCE	GAMMAINV
CORREL	GAMMALN
COUNT	GEOMEAN
COUNTA	GROWTH
COVAR	HARMEAN
CRITBINOM	HYPGEOMDIST
DEVSQ	INTERCEPT
EXPONDIST	KURT

Statistical (continued)

LARGE	QUARTILE
LINEST	RANDBETWEEN
LOGEST	RANK
LOGINV	RSQ
LOGNORMDIST	SKEW
MAX	SLOPE
MEDIAN	SMALL
MIN	STANDARDIZE
MODE	STDEV
NEGBINOMDIST	STDEVP
NORMDIST	STEYX
NORMINV	TDIST
NORMSDIST	TINV
NORMSINV	TREND
PEARSON	TRIMMEAN
PERCENTILE	TTEST
PERCENTRANK	VAR
PERMUT	VARP
POISSON	WEIBULL
PROB	ZTEST

Text

CHAR	EXACT
CLEAN	FIND
CODE	FIXED
CONCATENATE	LEFT
DOLLAR	LEN

Text (continued)

LOWER	SUBSTITUTE
MID	T
PROPER	TEXT
REPLACE	TRIM
REPT	UPPER
RIGHT	VALUE
SEARCH	

Part V:
Dummies Guide to Excel's Keyboard Commands

Mice are nice, but keys are a breeze. If you're sitting at the keyboard entering data, you'll lose valuable seconds by removing your hand from the keyboard, groping for the mouse, and then dragging it around looking for the right place to click.

After you get the hang of a few essential keyboard commands, you may find yourself using the mouse less and less. In any case, I've compiled the following lists of the most useful keyboard shortcuts.

Moving Through the Worksheet

Key (s)	Operation
Arrow keys (←, →, ↑, →)	Move left, right, up, down one cell
Home	Moves to the beginning of the row
PgUp	Moves up one screenful
Ctrl+PgUp	Moves to the previous sheet in a workbook
PgDn	Moves down one screenful
Ctrl+PgDn	Moves to the next sheet in a workbook
Ctrl+Home	Moves to the first cell in the worksheet (A1)
Ctrl+End	Moves to the last active cell of the worksheet
Ctrl+Arrow key	Moves to the edge of a data block; moves to the first nonblank cell if the cell is blank
Ctrl+Tab	Moves to the next window
Ctrl+Shift+Tab	Moves to the previous window
F5	Prompts for a cell address to go to

Selecting Cells in the Worksheet

Key (s)	Operation
Shift+Arrow key	Expands the selection in the direction indicated
Shift+spacebar	Selects the entire row
Ctrl+spacebar	Selects the entire column
Ctrl+Shift+spacebar	Selects the entire worksheet
Ctrl+A	Selects the entire worksheet
Shift+Home	Expands the selection to the beginning of the current row
Ctrl+*	Selects the block of data surrounding the active cell
F8	Extends the selection as you use navigation keys

Key (s)	Operation
Shift+F8	Adds other nonadjacent cells or ranges to the selection (pressing Shift+F8 again ends Add mode)
F5	Prompts for a range or range name to select

Moving Around Within a Range Selection

Key (s)	Operation
Enter	Moves the cell pointer to the next cell down in the selection
Shift+Enter	Moves the cell pointer to the previous cell up in the selection
Tab	Moves the cell pointer to the next cell to the right in the selection
Shift+Tab	Moves the cell pointer to the previous cell to the left in the selection
Ctrl+Period (.)	Moves to the next corner of the current cell range
Ctrl+Tab	Moves to the next cell range in a nonadjacent selection
Ctrl+Shift+Tab	Moves to the previous cell range in a nonadjacent selection
Shift+Backspace	Collapses the cell selection to just the active cell

Editing Keys in the Formula Bar

Key (s)	Operation
F2	Begins editing the active cell
Arrow keys	Move the cursor one character in the direction of the arrow

Key (s)	Operation
Shift+Arrow keys	Selects text
Home	Moves the cursor to the beginning of the line
End	Moves the cursor to the end of the line
Ctrl+Right arrow	Moves the cursor one word to the right
Ctrl+Left arrow	Moves the cursor one word to the left
Del	Deletes the character to the right of the cursor
Ctrl+Del	Deletes all characters from the cursor to the end of the line
Backspace	Deletes the character to the left of the cursor

Formatting Keys

Key (s)	Operation
Ctrl+1	Displays the Format Cells dialog box
Ctrl+B	Sets or removes boldface
Ctrl+I	Sets or removes italic
Ctrl+U	Sets or removes underlining
Ctrl+Shift+~	Applies the general number format
Ctrl+Shift+!	Applies the comma format with two decimal places
Ctrl+Shift+#	Applies the date format
Ctrl+Shift+$	Applies the currency format with two decimal places
Ctrl+Shift+%	Applies the percent format with no decimal places

Other Shortcut Keys

Key(s)	Operation
Ctrl+X	Edit⇔Cut command
Ctrl+Del	Edit⇔Cut command
Ctrl+C	Edit⇔Copy command
Ctrl+Ins	Edit⇔Copy command
Ctrl+V	Edit⇔Paste command
Shift+Ins	Edit⇔Paste command
Ctrl+Z	Edit⇔Undo command
Alt+Backspace	Edit⇔Undo command
Ctrl+R	Edit⇔Fill⇔Right command
Ctrl+D	Edit⇔Fill⇔Down command
Del	Edit⇔Clear⇔Contents command
Ctrl+S	File⇔Save command
Ctrl+F	Edit⇔Find command
Ctrl+H	Edit⇔Replace command
Ctrl+N	File⇔New command
Ctrl+O	File⇔Open command
Ctrl+P	File⇔Print command

Function Keys

Key(s)	Operation
F1	Help⇔Contents command
Shift+F1	Context-sensitive help
F2	Edit the active cell
Shift+F2	Insert⇔Note command
Ctrl+F2	Displays the Info Window
F3	Insert⇔Name⇔Paste command
Shift+F3	Insert⇔Function command

Key (s)	Operation
Ctrl+F3	Insert⇨Name⇨Define command
Ctrl+Shift+F3	Insert⇨Name⇨Create command
F4	Repeats the last action or changes cell reference while editing a formula
Shift+F4	Finds the next match
Ctrl+F4	File⇨Close command
Alt+F4	File⇨Exit command
Ctrl+Shift+F4	Finds the previous match
F5	Edit⇨Go To command
Shift+F5	Edit⇨Find command
Ctrl+F5	Restores a minimized document window to its previous size
F6	Moves to next pane in a split window
Shift+F6	Moves to previous pane in a split window
Ctrl+F6	Activates the next open window
Ctrl+Shift+F6	Activates the previous open window
F7	Starts the spelling checker
Ctrl+F7	Allows moving the current window with the arrow keys
F8	Toggles selection Extend mode on and off
Shift+F8	Toggles selection Add mode on and off
Ctrl+F8	Allows resizing of the current window with the arrow keys
F9	Recalculates all open worksheets
Shift+F9	Recalculates the current worksheet
Ctrl+F9	Minimizes the current window
F10	Activates the menu bar
Shift+F10	Activates the shortcut menu (simulates right-clicking)
Ctrl+F10	Maximizes the current window
F11	Insert⇨Chart⇨As New Sheet command
Shift+F11	Insert⇨Worksheet command

Key(s)	Operation
Ctrl+F11	Insert⇨Macro⇨MS Excel 4.0 Macro command
F12	File⇨Save As command
Shift+F12	File⇨Save command
Ctrl+F12	File⇨Open command
Ctrl+Shift+F12	File⇨Print command

Index

• U •

Notes

Notes